UPLIFTING AND MOTIVATIONAL STORIES FROM EXTRAORDINARY WOMEN

Inspirational Women of the World

Dawn Evans and Tracey Smolinski

+20 Inspirational Women

IWOW
INSPIRATIONAL WOMEN OF THE WORLD

Inspirational Women of the World

First published in 2020 by

Panoma Press Ltd

48 St Vincent Drive, St Albans, Herts, AL1 5SJ, UK
info@panomapress.com
www.panomapress.com

Book layout by Neil Coe.

978-1-784529-26-0

The rights of Dawn Evans and Tracey Smolinski to be identified as the authors of this work have been asserted in accordance with sections 77 and 78 of the Copyright, Designs and Patents Act 1988.

A CIP catalogue record for this book is available from the British Library.

This book is available online and in bookstores.

CONTENTS

INTRODUCTION
Dawn Evans and Tracey Smolinski   6

1. **CHOOSING GROWTH**
    Anita Lawrence   13

2. **THE MUSHER'S WIFE – PART ONE**
    Claire Rees   21

3. **INSPIRATION, RECOVERY AND
    ROLE MODELS**
    Emily Nuttall   31

4. **LANDMARKS AND LIGHTHOUSES**
    Emma Chivers   39

5. **GO FORWARD FEARLESSLY**
    Jan Mayfield   47

6. **RETRAIN THE BRAIN**
    Jenni Dunman   57

7.   FINDING JOY

Joy Whitlock   65

8.   NATURE'S GIFT

Karen Ramsay-Smith   73

9.   CONNECTING AGAIN

Kerry Martin   81

10.   MY LIFE MASK-FREE

LaChelle Adkins   89

11.   THE TRUTH OF IT

Leanne Eustace   97

12.   LIFE IS FOR LIVING

Lynsey Anne Toft   107

13.   LOVE TO LEAD

Melissa Curran   115

14. **TESTAMENT TO RESILIENCE**
    Rachel Brydon   123

15. **RAGS TO RICHES**
    Sandra Blake   131

16. **A MINDSET REVIVAL**
    Sheena Ytil   139

17. **WEIGHT NO MORE**
    Suzanne Burnell-Watts   147

18. **OVERCOMING ADVERSITY**
    Toni Clarkstone   155

19. **TO BE CONTINUED**
    Tracy Hill   163

20. **A BALANCING ACT**
    Vix Munro   171

INTRODUCTION

Dawn Evans and Tracey Smolinski are two powerhouses when it comes to business and female entrepreneurship.

With 25 years of business experience, numerous awards, qualifications, and high-net-worth clients, these women really know what they are doing. Only eight months ago they were both socialising with billionaire Sir Richard Branson on his private island.

Both regularly speak at business events: Dawn talks about her business growth strategies, and Tracey speaks about how to master networking, which is also the title of her best-selling book. They are often asked to share a platform, as their respective talks are complementary – networking and business growth go hand in hand. During the pandemic, Dawn and Tracey were invited to speak at the Global Stimulus Summit, where they spoke about the impact of the global pandemic and how they had taken their offline companies online. The summit also featured top entrepreneurs Les Brown, Sharon Lechter and Nik Halik.

Background

Dawn is chief executive of a multiple award-winning vocational training company, Ajuda Ltd; founder of Wales's biggest ever education and mental health shows; owner of Peak Coaching Academy and a published children's author. All these roles have helped develop her skills and experience as a successful entrepreneur. Dawn specialises in motivating, inspiring and helping startup and growing businesses develop. She has used her degree-level qualifications in education, sustainable leadership, and coaching and mentoring for entrepreneurial practice in developing and creating new entrepreneurs of the future.

Tracey Smolinski is chief executive of Wales' largest networking company, Introbiz. Like Dawn, she uses her wealth of business knowledge to mentor individuals on networking; she loves helping and developing people. Tracey's networking company has secured 3,000 global members, and has commissioned keynote speakers including Lord Sugar, Les Brown, Brian Tracy, Dr John Demartini, Grant Cardone, Hilary Devey, Baroness Michelle Mone, Sharon Lechter and many other renowned business people at her annual business expositions and online events.

Both women are also proud role models for the Welsh government's Big Ideas Wales programme, which involves going into schools and universities across the country to inspire confidence and motivate young adults to consider launching their own companies, empowering students and the entrepreneurs of the future.

Property investment is one of their other common interests, and they both love dogs, owning five between them. While Tracey has a love for the sea and has two holiday apartments by the coast in west Wales, Dawn loves mountains, and often spends her leisure time up a mountain or relaxing at her holiday home in rural France.

Between them, Dawn and Tracey have raised over £300k for charity because they thrive on helping other people by making a positive difference in their lives.

These women have made an impact and have worked with many budding and growing entrepreneurs across the globe, who now run successful businesses too. They thrive on watching others succeed.

So why IWOW and the book?

Let us take you back to 2012 when the women first met. Tracey hosted a networking event, which Dawn attended as a delegate. She bought a ticket to a seminar in London a month later, which was delivered by Kevin Green, a serial entrepreneur and star of *The Secret Millionaire*, a reality television show. After that, Kevin invited Tracey to London to host a post-event cocktail party, where Tracey and Dawn first met. They got on well from the start and built up a good rapport. A few months later, Dawn joined Tracey's network, Introbiz, and that was the start of a great friendship.

Little did they know what that would lead to years later.

Over the years, Tracey and Dawn often met to discuss their businesses and come up with ideas for each other. They had fun in the process. In spring 2019, they were sitting in a hotel in Penarth, Wales with their husbands, having a few drinks, when Dawn mentioned that she wanted to create a ladies' conference. Tracey offered to do it with her. Dawn thought it was a great idea to collaborate, so they launched the conference just two months later. It was a great success.

In March 2020, after the novel coronavirus (Covid-19) outbreak had been declared a pandemic, Tracey and Dawn pivoted their businesses and decided to take the conference online. To make it an online success, they needed an online audience, so they set up a Facebook group, Inspirational Women of the World. More than 3,000 women joined the group within six weeks.

They noticed that many of the women had imposter syndrome and were lacking in business knowledge and confidence. They realised that these women would benefit from the online conference, which was a great success, as well as from Dawn and Tracey's expertise, guidance and support. So, in June 2020, they formed IWOW Ltd.

Many ideas came from IWOW. As well as wanting to create a global community of female entrepreneurs, Dawn and Tracey also wanted to give women an opportunity to tell their stories and be heard by a wider audience. So, they set out to find 20 inspirational women to feature in this book, each with her own chapter, and her own story. Once you start reading it, you will be fascinated by their stories and will surely agree that they truly are inspirational women of the world.

Dawn and Tracey now have a mission: to make a huge impact by inspiring and uplifting one million women by 2030.

They are planning and organising their third annual women's conference, which will be hosted in London on 2 July 2021.

Other opportunities will include retreats, workshops and mastermind challenges. Thanks to their connections around the world, they are also creating opportunities further afield – from socialising with Sir Richard Branson on his private island (which they were fortunate to experience in 2019), to building a village on a Moroccan mountain to help poor women set up their own business.

The Moroccan project is scheduled to start in September 2021, and every year they intend to add a new building. By year 10, this will be a business village where women can create businesses that they would not otherwise have been able to – and what a difference this will make for these women of Morocco. This is what IWOW is all about: empowering women, lifting them and giving them opportunities that they would not have thought possible.

Dawn and Tracey are also confident that when they help women connect, these women will excel and lift one another, and have friendships for life too.

If you would like to find out more about the IWOW community, or you would like to join, please get in touch by emailing hello@iwowglobal.com Dawn and Tracey would love to hear from you.

The proceeds of this book will be used to help build the village in Morocco. To donate to the village, and be part of something extraordinary, please visit www.iwowglobal.com

Join our community!

http://bit.ly/3d6SVbZiwow

Dawn Evans

---

https://www.ajuda.org.uk

https://www.peakcoachingacademy.com

https://www.linkedin.com/in/ajudadawn/

Tracey Smolinski

---

http://introbiz.co.uk

https://www.linkedin.com/in/introbiz/

1.
CHOOSING GROWTH

Anita Lawrence

Over the past two decades of my career in people development, I have been asked these questions repeatedly in my training sessions, personal friendships and work relationships:

"Why can't I achieve what I want in life, despite working so hard every day?"

"Why is my boss (or kid or teen or spouse) so difficult to understand?"

"Why am I always the one going through so many challenges?"

"Why do I still feel dissatisfied and empty, despite having achieved my goals?"

"I have everything I want in life, but something is missing. What do you think I'm missing?"

These are adversities in different shapes and forms. I love the quote by Mark Twain "The two most important days in your life are the day you are born and the day you find out why." I am honoured to share my story on how adversity paved the way to find my 'why'.

I'm an easy-going person, born and raised in a loving family. I grew up believing that if I followed the rules and did not step on anyone's toes, life would turn out all right. When I was growing up, I looked up to my dad; he was my role model, living boldly and always making a difference, wherever he went. I admired him for his strength, resilience, optimism, confidence and boldness; everything I wish I'd had growing up. I always felt secure, protected and assured that all will go well with me, as long as I had my dad to fall back on. We were close. But life turned out very differently.

My very first and greatest loss in life happened when I was 20: my dad died of a sudden heart attack. He was travelling out of town and collapsed before he could board the bus. We didn't find out until the next day. My whole world collapsed. "Why, God? Why did you take my dad away? Why this way? Who was going to walk me down the aisle on my wedding day?" These were some of the questions I struggled with for an entire year. I remember crying to the song 'Butterfly Kisses' by Bob Carlisle, a beautiful song about a father and his daughter.

At the end of that year, my mum, my greatest cheerleader, spoke with such love, wisdom and insight, having given me some time to grieve the loss of my dad. Being a nurse, she appreciated the fact that my dad had died without any prolonged suffering or pain. She understood the possibility of him having suffered a stroke and ending up bedridden. I recall now that I had not been able to empathise with her for her loss, because my grief was too overwhelming.

In her wisdom, she asked me, "Would you rather your dad had died instantly of a heart attack or that he'd suffered a stroke and been bedridden for years?" Then she asked, "What blessing do you see as a result of his death?"

I did not like the first question at all and responded very quickly. "He should have collapsed at home," I replied. "I could have called the ambulance and you could have performed CPR and he would have survived."

My mum then said in a calm voice, "That's not an option; pick from the ones I gave you."

I thought long and hard and began to think of what my dad would have preferred. Without a doubt, it was the first option. My dad, an active man, lived an adventurous life. He would never have wanted to live at all if it meant him not being able to live out loud. I finally understood why option one was indeed a blessing.

As for the second question, my mum reminded me that life is like a coin – you have both heads and tails (blessings and pain or positives and negatives). You can CHOOSE a side to focus on and live the rest of your life with everything that side of the coin offers. If you choose to focus on the pain, that's what you get more of. I know this because for one whole year, tears were my best friend. I had memories of crying myself to sleep many nights, holding a picture of my dad and replaying all our moments spent together, the laughter we shared and the countless conversations we had: the fun, good and serious ones. I remembered everything he had taught me, his encouraging words and, most of all, his belief in me. I focused on how lonely I was with a part of my life taken away from me. I lost the interest to hang out with friends and enjoy a good laugh. I remember working full-time and attending night classes in college to keep me moving forward and distracted. Nothing else mattered to me then.

What were the blessings I received as a result of my dad's death? It took me some time to figure this out. I became more mature; I exercised my independence to make decisions for my future. I stopped taking people for granted and began valuing them more than ever before. I began to appreciate and cherish LIFE – mine and others' – in a very different light, knowing that the only time I really have with someone is TODAY. I began to give my 100% for myself and for others. I began to look at the positive side of life, to move me in the direction of my goals and dreams. My empathy towards people who lost their loved ones increased tremendously. I hold on to these life lessons, to this day.

My passion for people has increased since then and I have continually been finding ways to help people live their best lives, personally and professionally. I found my purpose early in life. I realised that equipping people and seeing them live life to the full gave me great satisfaction and fulfilment.

> ## "You like someone for who they are. You love someone because of who you are."
>
> **Anita Lawrence**

Everyone wants to have a meaningful and happy life, loving family, fulfilling career, peace of mind and a life purpose, but how many are ready, willing and eager to start taking the necessary steps to get what they desire? We must make the decision and have the discipline to live it out. Growing in character is crucial for success.

I believe we can grow more through pain when we have the right focus and perspective.

I have discovered that many people can achieve their success when they possess three prerequisites that set a strong foundation for growth: self-awareness; valuing themselves; and being willing to acknowledge their blind spots and change through feedback from others.

Once you have built your strong foundation, three key ingredients are needed to achieve success:

First, a community. Who is your community? Do you have people who affirm and encourage you? People who remind you of who you can become? People who see your potential, before you can see it? People who love you unconditionally while helping you see your blind spots? I was blessed to have such people in my life during my early years as a young adult. Now, I have a loving, supportive husband and a best friend who are part of that community. I deliberately look for the best in people and make a point of telling them of the potential and beauty I see in them. Someone complimented me by calling me a 'gold-digger' because I was quick to see the gold in others and dig it out.

Second, a coaching relationship. Do you have someone who asks you questions that help you reflect and make you aware of areas in your life that need change? Finding answers within yourself will lead you to a place of better decision-making and transformation. I underwent coaching and it was one of the best decisions I made in life. It came with a price, and it was worth it.

Third, accountability. When deciding to grow any area of your life, sharing that with someone who cares for you helps you hold yourself accountable for your decision and action. I have seen major differences between people who have accountability partners and those who don't. I believe we all have good intentions but that does not guarantee good results. Accountability bridges the gap between your good intentions and your actions. Find an accountability partner today.

My growth for success started with adversity. I developed self-awareness, followed by continual growth and then transformation into a leader who develops other leaders. This is an ongoing journey for me. I believe that our world needs us to step up every day and make a positive difference wherever we are. 'Choosing Growth,' even through adversities has been my motto in life. I believe without growth, we can't achieve success. Are you ready to start your growth to success today?

"Lead with vision, inspire with heart, live the example."

Anita Lawrence

Anita Lawrence

Anita Lawrence is a certified speaker, trainer and coach with the John Maxwell Team. She founded Exceed Excellence, a training and consulting company, and has 20 years' experience in the people development and transformation areas. Anita was certified in the US as a personality trainer in 2000 under the late Florence Littauer, and is an active practitioner of the Personality Plus transformational tool.

Anita aids personal and professional growth through life-changing programmes, conducting workshops and conferences, delivering keynote speeches and coaching. She motivates leaders, teams and organisations to reach their desired goals by building strong partnerships.

Anita's passion for people complements her burning desire to see them succeed to be the best version of themselves. She fulfils her life's mission by building communities of leaders worldwide to positively impact nations. Anita enjoys travelling the world and appreciates the individuality of different cultures.

www.facebook.com/Anita.Lawrence.JMT/
www.linkedin.com/in/anita-lawrence-jmt
www.exceed-excellence.com

IWOW
INSPIRATIONAL WOMEN OF THE WORLD

2.
THE MUSHER'S WIFE – PART ONE

Claire Rees

I was born in Ynysmaerdy, a little village lying at the head of the Rhondda Fach Valley in Wales. Staying in was not an option in those days and I was a tomboy; I loved wearing my wellies and jeans, although I also loved singing and dancing (the dancing was really good, but the singing was bad – nothing has really changed).

I am married, for the second time, with three children: my biological son and two stepchildren.

I co-founded Wildspirit Dog Sledding with my husband, and we own the Introbiz Sweden franchise, a business-to-business networking events company.

My son was born when I was 21. This was the life I was destined to have, and I was quite comfortable, until my partner and I split up when James was just four. Having left school with no qualifications, I had to decide whether to live on welfare benefits or start studying.

I decided on bettering myself for the future and to become qualified, and from the age of 24 until I was 30, I studied teacher training to degree level, and project management.

When my son's father and I split up, I misguidedly thought that it was his job to support us. At the beginning I was 'that mum' who thought I could control their relationship, but I realised that my son needed his dad. Although there was some conflict about bringing up our son, as is normal, James now has the relationship he deserves with both his parents.

Everything I have ever done has been with James in mind. I wanted to be a good role model for him, although I have made some mistakes (sorry buddy). The biggest challenge in my life was when he became distant towards me. I was hurt, but my mother-in-law guided me. She said I should keep the door open, that he would fly back when he was ready, and he did.

It's the most satisfying job to see how my James has turned out today: he is my doppelgänger.

During my 20s and 30s, I built my career, brought up my son, got married, divorced and bought and sold a few houses.

I would say that during this time, I thought I was indestructible. I hid my feelings and I wasn't very good at expressing myself wisely. I was the strong one, so I didn't allow myself to look weak. I ignored those warning signs in my heart.

I loved investing my time and energy into helping people improve themselves. I know this was hypocritical, as I didn't do the same for me. I am not, and never was, good at giving gifts and cards, but my energy and what I have to give to people is my gift. I have helped many people with their lifestyles and health, and I have encouraged people to do things they have never ever done before, believing in people to reach their full potential.

Jumping forward to the sexy bit in my life – I met my match in my second husband. He is a typical mountain man. If you saw some of the things he has got me into, it's crazy, but this is why I have a story to tell.

We emigrated to Sweden, Richard in 2011 followed by me in 2012. We hadn't done any research, but my brother-in-law lived there, so that was enough for me. I had always wanted to emigrate, so I did. Typical of me, I want to do something, and I made it happen – isn't it amazing how it works out in the end? I am a lot wiser these days, but only through experience. It's good to be carefree and take risks, but you have to be wise and learn from mistakes you have made in the past.

Richard found us a wilderness cabin. It was my dream, a log cabin 850m up on the side of a mountain, five hours south of the Arctic Circle, with no water and no electricity. We had an outside toilet, just like the story character Heidi.

We started our dog sledding business – it's quite crazy now to think how we managed, and made it work.

Imagine after a full day's work, coming home to your cabin and it's minus 5C; you then have the equivalent of another full-time job to warm up the cabin and get things done in the evening.

Even though these were tough times, and I honestly have no idea how we did it, they were the best times of our life. There is nothing quite like the quietness and peacefulness when you live in the scenic mountains.

Richard had difficulties getting access to his daughter, and every week would be stressful, a fight just to speak with her. We applied to court and even after this, the manipulation that he and his daughter endured throughout this time put a lot of pressure on all the family.

From my experience, I have seen at first-hand how a child can suffer. Children should never be used as ammunition – they deserve to be children.

I am so proud of what Richard and I have accomplished through this journey together. Our relationship with Freja is amazing when she is with us. However, when she is at her mother's house, she is a different child, which is heart-breaking.

During this time, we struggled financially. Sometimes there was only a tin of tuna in the cupboard, and no food to feed our dogs. Many times, we thought that it was over.

Richard and I are the type of people who never give up and we pushed ourselves through it – even bagging ourselves a TV documentary with Kevin McCloud in 2014.

After the success of the TV documentary, we had to change our lifestyle for the business. We moved to a quaint tourist village called Ottsjö and that is where we are today. Living with our 80 sled dogs, Jämtland's largest kennel, and still living our dream. The cabin life will always be a goal for us, and never forgotten.

Richard's son Joe came to live with us in 2016 and this was quite a squeeze because we then lived in a one-bedroom apartment. Joe was 16 at the time, and not without problems, which we slowly overcame. He is now growing into an independent, confident young man.

Tourism with the dogs is amazing. It's a dream come true for some, and we are privileged that this is what we deliver, but for only six months of the year.

The rest of the time we have to catch up and look for other work, which becomes tedious.

In 2019, I was suffering emotionally, and I knew it was time to take part in self-development and invest in myself. I contacted my good friend Tracey Smolinski and arranged a catch-up when I was next in Wales; she connected me to my mastermind coach Adam Strong. By attending mastermind challenges, and subjecting myself to online networking events, I started to grow and develop.

Within a few months I was investing in Tracey's business, Introbiz, as a franchisee, setting up Introbiz Sweden.

I have learned that networking, investing in yourself and finding your tribe of support is just as important in your life and business as marketing.

I know that if I hadn't taken this step, I would have been likely to fail in life. My motivation would have waned and my anxiety and depression would have deepened.

One of the biggest things I have learned in my life is that if you acknowledge your problems they can be dealt with, but when you ignore them, they will build up, until – guess what – you reach breakdown point. This is when life forced me to deal with my issues and I started to grow. When I didn't deal with them, I just crashed, burned out and became anxious.

I am in a much better place, and I can see and feel so much more positivity and success in my life.

Here is my gift to you, based on my life lessons:

- What other people think of you is none of your business.

- Work with people who want to work with you.

- Be as kind as you can, and give what you can, but do not be afraid to say, "No."

- Trust your instincts.

- Develop and look after yourself.

- Solve your problems but remember you cannot change other people's minds if they believe they are correct; deal with it.

- Have a faith that you can turn to for guidance.

- You cannot control people coming into or out of your life, but you can be the best you can be.

- Attract the lovely people who want to be around you.

- Look at other income streams.

- Do not be afraid to approach people – the worst they can say is, "No."

- Be open, transparent and trustworthy.

- Don't overthink.

- Your opinions are always different from others' opinions.

- Know your abilities.

- Live up to your own expectations, not those of others.

- Trust.

- You can live your life only through your own experiences.

Lots of Welsh love from Sweden

Claire Rees

Claire Rees

Claire's background is in health, fitness and project management and she has developed many successful projects for the public sector in Wales. Claire loves the great outdoors, and during her life in Wales she trained as a mountain leader and organised trips to the Welsh mountains, as well as climbing the Six Peaks Challenge mountains while carrying a rowing machine.

Claire and her husband, Richard, own a tourism business and networking franchise in Sweden.

Claire loves meeting people and working to meet their needs. She believes that when people book a trip of a lifetime with her, that is what they deserve to get. She spends a lot of time and effort making sure that everybody is happy and satisfied.

Claire is a natural problem-solver and loves to serve people's needs. She is hypersensitive to moods and feelings, and loves self-development and psychology.

www.facebook.com/welshsweden
www.linkedin.com/in/claire-rees-4062a3a6/
www.introbizsweden.se
www.wildspirit.se

3.
INSPIRATION, RECOVERY AND ROLE MODELS

Emily Nuttall

Setting the scene

When I was a child in primary school, my teacher asked me to picture the people in my life who I looked up to for guidance and support. Those who offered me protection and safety from harm, along with encouragement, love and care. How these people would be that positive voice of hope and help me grow, develop and strive through the challenges of unknown fears and events that life would bring. Most of the other children imagined celebrities or TV stars; for me it was three remarkable women in my family who have made me the Emily I am today.

Inspiration and recovery

I could never have imagined when I came into this world that life was going to throw me the adversities of cerebral palsy from the age of one – a disability resulting from injury to my brain while my mother was pregnant that affected my physical movement and development. I was born prematurely at 24 weeks. When I was three, I was very curious about what was happening to me. Asking lots of questions, I drove my parents and family crazy. I was already going to face so many unknowns in my life. I was having to adapt to the physical challenges of my cerebral palsy and the many hurdles I had to clear to reach the many different milestones that other three-year-olds were already achieving.

In September 1996, I was embarking on my new adventure of preschool – something that my family and the professionals supporting me thought may not be possible with my cerebral palsy. However, against the odds, I was able to embark on this opportunity. The preschool offered an open, homely environment, laid out beautifully with the surroundings of an extraordinary garden with plenty of nature that could be observed from every window. To allow me to be a part of every preschool opportunity, I had to accept and understand I was going to need intense support. This is where my first remarkable role model became part of my journey.

Nan was a fitness fanatic, an energetic and smiling lady known as Chris. She had very curly brown hair, an infectious smile that would make me feel better and she gave the best hugs in the world. This allowed me to feel loved and comforted, just as though I were being hugged by my brown, fluffy teddy bear. I was so young, trying to make sense of the world, but Nan was patient; she would listen openly, never letting me give up, no matter what the challenge may have been with my physical disability. Most importantly, she believed in helping me grow through disability sports, enabling me to feel included within society.

I remember sitting one day, with my array of brightly coloured pencils and drawing pads in front of me, the sun shining beautifully through the cottage windows and colourful flowers on view. I drew myself, mummy and daddy holding hands with smiling faces, like any other little girl my age, then I imagined I was in a fairy tale, that we would live together forever happily ever after, as in the films. Sadly, my father walked out when I was three; he chose a new life and family. My father figure, who I had bonded with so closely, ripped my world apart.

My father was now living a new life. I was no longer the three-year-old little girl without any fear or worry in the world. I was now 15 and many changes had happened. My father's new home was a frightening place where I regularly witnessed domestic violence between my father and stepmother. I experienced emotional abuse as well. My stepmother couldn't accept me for having a physical disability and for looking 'different' from my siblings.

She didn't want me to be a part of her 'normal' family because I would ruin it, being a burden. Ingrained so deeply in my mind like a scar that never fades, were the words she called me: 'failure', 'useless', 'worthless', 'a mistake', 'fat' and 'ugly'. I was told I would never be loved and would be excluded, away from everyone. This was a constant vicious cycle of treatment I received and I believed every single word. I desperately needed control. I could cope with feeling physical pain as I did with cerebral palsy as a way of blocking out my feelings.

Self-harm and anorexia became that control. Controlling my food, weight, body image and shape became that release, as I had lost all other control, physically and emotionally, in my life. I needed to block out the stabbing of the emotional pain and distress; I was ashamed to be the Emily I was, confused, broken and bruised, not knowing if I was loved anymore.

Gran was another very special role model in my life. Called Molly, she was a petite lady with grey, curly hair. She was an incredible primary school and music teacher, patient and caring. I entrusted her with what I was experiencing at my father's and stepmother's house. The relationship with my own mother was broken; I was lost, angry, scared and going off the rails, but Gran, with her calming nature and words, was always close by, like a guardian angel on my shoulder hugging me. She would keep me safe, making everything OK – my mental health, the eating disorder, my disability, and with family intervention teams, she helped hold everything together.

Auntie was my final role model, and someone I aspired to be like. Her name was Meg. She was my musical inspiration and a teacher. Meg was petite too, but had a warming voice. She helped me to understand and make sense of the world. She encouraged and inspired my creative talents, helping me to develop into a confident, intellectual woman through writing, music, dance and art. Like my gran and nan, she kept the family together and me safe from harm, helping me to achieve anything I set my mind to, which helped me to make sense of the world I was living in.

My three role models are sadly not with me in this world anymore, which is painfully hard. They were taken so unexpectedly and in very distressing situations; I often carry that blame and trauma for their deaths, but my memories of them and their voices never go away.

Often in my life now there are huge amounts of pain, fear, trauma, despair, frightening flashbacks from my past and what life still throws my way – my physical disabilities, life events, anorexia, family breakdowns, trauma and mental health. However, I'm reassured and comforted by my three special family members. Their voices overpower the distressing voices of my past abuser and anorexia. Even though it is like a violent war inside my head, they give me resilience, strength and hope.

In my work as a disability sports coach and campaigner, MOE foundation coach, mental health and eating disorder campaigner, media volunteer, speaker, author and champion, I'm now a role model for countless people out there facing physical and mental health adversities. I campaign for equal rights for disabilities and inclusive opportunities through sporting activities, coaching individuals to achieve their full potential. I work with children and young people, helping them understand those with disabilities, so they can learn and be inspired by the amazing individuals who show what they can still achieve, in spite of their disabilities.

I coach and connect others to become the best they can be and feel supported in the community. I help children and young people find safe places they can call home, so that they know they are loved and wanted. I help keep families together, to prevent family breakdowns and help keep young people safe. I am determined to see that all those facing a mental health problem are supported and heard, and openly share my mental health struggles. I am the voice that isn't afraid to speak out to make sure others can access treatment just as I did. I inspire governments and members of our community to be role models to our societies today, making sure that treatment is accessible and available when anyone may need it. I write and I speak openly and honestly, in the hope that my words bring reassurance and comfort, so that you are not alone, that you have hope. I am a champion for change.

I have been out of in-patient treatment for my anorexia, mental health and disabilities for three years now. Five years ago, I would never have dreamed that possible, given how ill I was, and that I had been told I wouldn't make it. It makes me incredibly proud of myself, and I still fight so hard at recovery. I always pick myself back up, fighting against the odds; I'm determined to break free of my demons fully, for good, even when I'm still faced with many challenges, pain and despair. I will not be the victim of my anorexia, abuser, trauma, disability and mental health struggles – I'm a survivor. I have learned that the key to this is not being afraid to be vulnerable or to ask for help, as it shows great strength.

We all need and can be a role model – whether we are a charity worker, a loved one, a coach or a professional – to offer guidance, strength and support, so we can inspire and grow to help others and ourselves to be that best that we can be.

Be that voice who's proud to be heard, to help save and change someone's life. I believe this is the Emily who is creating a positive, healthy, happy future for others and myself. All tunnels do have a light at the end of them, which I can slowly see and feel, and that is truly beautiful.

Emily Nuttall

Emily Nuttall is a motivational disability and mental health campaigner, champion and speaker. She is a disability sports coach with Guernsey Mobility Let's Go, a MOE foundation coach, an entrepreneur and inspirational author of *It's Ok to Not Be Ok*. As well as raising funds for Beat, the UK's eating disorder charity, she works as a community connector for Health Connections; as a Time to Change Champion; as a media volunteer for Mind; and as an ambassador for Action for Children, helping keep families together and prevent homelessness.

Emily was diagnosed with cerebral palsy at the age of one and is an inspirational woman who has overcome adversity. From the age of 12, she has struggled with anxiety, depression, self-harm, suicidal thoughts and anorexia, and is a survivor of domestic violence and emotional abuse.

Emily is embarking on sports coaching and disability studies, coaching development and psychology, building on her studies in health and social care and previous employment with children and young people through the Guernsey Youth Commission. She has undertaken Adult Mental Health First Aid and Youth Mental Health First Aid courses, and has completed domestic violence awareness training. She is passionate about helping support children, young people and adults who go through similar situations. Her mission is to empower them to be the best that they can be, and to show them that anything is possible.

www.emilynuttall.com   @emily4993

INSPIRATIONAL WOMEN OF THE WORLD

4.
LANDMARKS AND LIGHTHOUSES

Emma Chivers

Abstract

This chapter provides an overview of key 'landmarks' that have been significant during my personal and educational journey. It outlines the challenges faced and explains how key individuals provided support and guidance, while helping me to overcome obstacles during my complex journey. I describe these individuals as 'lighthouses', metaphorically, as they have provided light and direction during troublesome times. Second, it describes the lessons learned and the actions taken to prevent the issues from recurring. They are an informal guide, which can be used to help you navigate and steer your own journey, regardless of your destination.

Where to begin

I was unsure where to start my journey as there were several landmarks I could have included. The following are significant. My childhood and adolescence were not atypical, and I finished school without any qualifications. This landmark left my future looking bleak. My teenage life was not easy and there were significant landmarks that had an impact upon my education and transition into adulthood. After leaving home at 17, I worked in the hospitality industry, travelling from one location to another, before getting married at 19 and returning to my hometown to work in manufacturing. After a few years, I was keen to escape.

Two years later, I plucked up the courage to meet my previous youth worker, who managed adult education provision, for some advice on how I could return to education. It was a meeting I would always remember, as I was asked to write 500 words about 'something that was important to me'. Writing about the life and death of a young boy who had been failed by society and systems, was emotionally challenging, and made me write from the heart. This, my first piece of written work since leaving formal education, was notable for the lack of capital letters, paragraph breaks and punctuation marks. I wish I had kept it to show myself and others how far I have travelled. As an academic, it makes me smile, and I use the story to inspire and reassure students as they nervously embark upon their own journeys. This significant landmark contributed to the direction of my professional career, as a youth and community worker, and my one and only GCSE in English language. I could never have estimated the impact of that initial meeting on my educational and professional trajectory.

During my early 30s, other significant landmarks that threatened my educational journey included the deaths of two immediate family members, as well as severe mental health issues and alcoholism, which were rife in my close family. This was also the time when I got divorced, which changed the direction of my personal life. These detrimental experiences occurred during my final year at university, leading me to question whether I could juggle the competing demands and commitments of being a single mum to three-year-old twins, working full-time and studying. As I considered leaving university, my lecturer was the 'shining light' who managed to guide and support me while I attempted to navigate my way around these obstacles, which undoubtedly prevented me dropping out.

I continued to juggle the challenges and demands of working full time as a senior youth officer and went on to achieve a postgraduate certificate in education. Another string to my bow, this equipped me to deliver youth and community work training, as well as providing additional finances to significantly reduce financial pressure.

During my late 30s and early 40s, I still experienced several significant challenges: ending a long-term relationship, being a lone parent to teenage twins, and managing and juggling finances with little or no family support. My shining lights during this time were two friends and a family member who helped me with childcare so that I could maintain my high-profile job in a local authority.

A key educational landmark that altered the direction of my professional life was the completion of a master's degree in youth and community development, as I secured my dream job as a senior lecturer at a local university. This gave me an opportunity to develop further, educationally and professionally, and also for me to educate and support those students who were nervous and anxious as they commenced their own educational and professional journeys.

As I reach the 'big 50', I am an academic subject manager and senior lecturer at a university and have completed five years of a professional doctorate. For a girl who left school with no qualifications, I am almost there.

Having outlined some of the key landmarks that have contributed to my journey and current destination, in the following section I give an overview of the lessons that I have learned and would like to share.

Lessons learned

Reflecting on the educational, personal and professional landmarks that have influenced my journey required me to go back to reassure and comfort that young woman of 16 who failed all her GCSEs. To put my arms around her, to tell her – and other young people – that your personal and family background does not have to dictate and direct the rest of your life. You can set your own goals and ambitions and go for it. Seek those individuals who look after and care about you, and metaphorically, use their shining lights, to guide, direct and support you. These 'lighthouses' will help you to navigate your personal and educational journey. You need a range of different individuals who can help and support you to overcome key challenges in every aspect of your life, personal and professional. This will help you navigate a way through the major challenges that threaten to throw you off course and prevent you from reaching your destination.

Education can transform your life and help you achieve independence. However, not everyone will understand that, and some people will try to steer you away from your chosen destination. Make sure you know what direction you want to take (getting some good advice from a careers adviser or an educational representative); identify your aspirations and goals; and compile a plan on how you want to reach them. Write them down and stick to them; no matter how big or small, they will help you get to where you want to be.

Think about your 'lighthouses' – who are those individuals who can help you overcome and manage any significant challenges and obstacles? Your qualification is your end goal, and whether it's an occupational or formal qualification you have in mind, not every individual in your life will see the importance or relevance of you succeeding. Remember this. You will need to put yourself first and identify times, opportunities and activities that will help you succeed. Make a plan and stick to it.

Use the resources available to you. For example, if your goal is to achieve an educational qualification, make sure you know about the support mechanisms available to you. These may include disability support, study skills resources and personal tutors, for example. Make sure you access them. Do not forget that having sufficient time to achieve your goal or target is essential.

When you identify an issue or a problem, do not just sit on it. Reflect on the issue or problem and try to resolve it. If you are unable to do this, look for your 'lighthouse', that key person who can guide and support you during a difficult and challenging time. These actions will help keep you focused and heading in the right direction, instead of moving off course.

There are other obstacles that have slowed me down or prevented me from reaching my destination. These can be personal and or family relationships. Relationships can be complex, time-consuming and draining. Occasionally, they can put obstacles in your way, which are not always easy to see. When you are entering into a new personal relationship, take your time and do not jump in with both feet. Remember, this is about looking after yourself – once you are in a relationship, and you have an emotional and physical connection, it is not that easy to get out.

Think about your relationships. Who is that trusted friend or family member who can guide, support and direct you here, your 'lighthouse'? Before embarking upon a relationship, devise a checklist of items that are important to you – I know that this seems harsh, but this is about you, and you are important. What are you looking for in a relationship? What is important to you, at this stage in your life? Values, principles, personality, intelligence, looks (yes, they may also be important for you), education? Are they emotionally intelligent – would they give you a cuddle (or a cwtch, in Wales) when you need one? Remember, this person is going to be spending a significant amount of time with you and sharing your life, so compile your list and make an informed decision.

Emma Chivers

Emma Chivers is a consultant and researcher who specialises in youth and community work, higher education, social and public policy and young people. She is also a runner, single mum, executive coach and mentor. Emma has worked as a senior manager in higher education and a senior lecturer in youth and community work.

She is currently undertaking her professional doctorate in social and public policy. As a non-traditional academic, she is determined to reduce barriers to participation in higher education, and is committed to informing policy developments and influencing change.

Emma is chair of Youth Cymru, a national youth work charity, and is a professionally qualified youth and community worker, with more than 25 years' experience. She has participated in European and international work, coordinating international student visits to Moving Mountains Trust in Kenya and visiting community groups in Sudan on behalf of the British Council and Women Making a Difference.

www.linkedin.com/in/emma-chivers-33250b28

5.
GO FORWARD FEARLESSLY

Jan Mayfield

"Are you ready to turn off the life support machine?" Those words echoed in the distance. He died, leaving me with two young children. After this, I rebuilt my life and retrained to be a teacher to support and look after our girls.

Teaching became a passion; to watch people grow and develop from one area to another is like seeing the lights being switched on in a dark room.

Balancing being a single parent with working life and fitting in the gym, I was in a particularly good place. Until one day when…

Bang!

We crashed!

A car accident left me with a medical condition called fibromyalgia, which was rarely heard of in those days. It took me out of my life for two solid years. I would crawl out of bed to see the girls off to school, then try to stay awake and pain-free for the rest of the day. I would set an alarm for the time they were due home.

It is amazing what you can hide for a few hours.

Eventually, ill health meant giving up my passion, the job I loved: teaching.

Did I really love that job?

Or was it what I knew I loved – was it that it was time to embrace my soul's life purpose and reason for being on Earth?

I had always been a little different. I have many memories of being told, as a child, "Don't be silly; your imagination is running away with you." I know now for sure that it was not. I do see things differently from how many people do, and over the years have embraced my spirituality and uniqueness. My innate intuitive visions are celebrated now.

"Go and live your life," the rheumatologist said sternly as I left his clinically decorated white room and looked back to say, "Thank you." Feeling the pain in my body, I was searching for a way out of this. My world was closing in on me and I seemed unable to do anything about it.

"Go and live your life." How dare he?

A Native American proverb came to mind, "Judge no man before you have walked for two moons in his moccasins."

I scurried in slow motion along the corridor, but that day changed my life. Sometimes there are pivotal points, and this was one of them. I call them catalysts.

"I am going to show you how I can live *my* life," I remember thinking.

Everything we encounter is *for* us to encounter, I believe. This was proving rather difficult though. I did sink into a deep depression, resulting in two suicide attempts. I now know that these attempts were not conscious thoughts; they just happened. Some evidence of this is in my book, *Zoetic Soul: Pertaining to Life. Your Life.*

With two growing children, no job, little money and a whole lot of positivity, I needed a plan of action. But how could I, when taking a shower left me exhausted – and that was without washing my hair – and chronic fatigue stopped me in my tracks. I swung between crying, sobbing and being positive most days.

Have you ever had holistic healing?

I started visiting a healer and reflexologist, and week after week I would go. She never understood why I needed it every week. After six months my pattern began to change; I started to need it less often and eventually visiting her monthly.

Light bulb moment!

"This stuff is working…"

"I am fearless."

I slowly began to take more action to recovery. "I am not this illness, and it will not define me," I used to chant this around my home.

Many emotions rose in me – fear, being scared, feeling guilty and being uncomfortable – all dispelled as I worked through them. They needed to show themselves to take me to the next place in my life.

Changing what I ate and walking a few extra steps a day began to have positive results.

I soon learned the art of self-talk, strategies to move forward one small step at a time and little tricks, to trick my mind into thinking I was well – "I am, aren't I?"

I used to take myself away from the pain by transforming it in my mind to become a flower – I was blooming in a new direction, just as the flower pushes out through the ground when the seed germinates. I, too, was doing this and I lived as though I were in full bloom, with a vibrant flower head and beautiful petals – not pain.

To rebuild everything in your life is no easy task. The doctors often dismiss you, while other people look and say, "But you look fine."

"Get inside my body," I used to think, but got fed up with saying it.

"Get on with it Jan – you can do this!"

I will share with you how you too can help yourself, no matter what your problems are. I have given an example, with that illness, but it could easily be a relationship break-up, loss of a loved one, depression or some other traumatic event.

The event is a catalyst for change – always remember that.

The road to the end – I smile as I type – the end is the death bed, the soul transitioning, and the road is your journey to get there.

Constantly, evolving and growing.

Sprouting new ideas and trampling through the waters that are often muddy from others' actions.

You know you must never react to the actions of others.

The actions of others are simply that: their actions, their choice.

Let us clear the waters – we need to be crystal clear in all that we do to allow our inner selves to shine.

To build a rod of steel inside is key to moving on – this is a pivotal point that you will always come back to.

We must let go of the conditioning we have learned from the media, from our parents (with the best intentions, but decades out of date), and from society in general. In the main, these do not serve the unique you.

We need to specifically let go from in the womb to seven years old. Yes, I said in the womb. I believe you hear in this space and may carry thoughts from people around you. Many of my clients have released from this time, with my help in identifying at what age they were holding on to, and they soon found inner freedom once this was done.

We let go by cutting the emotional ties that no longer serve us, by letting go of illness or traumatic events, so that they do not define us. You are not the event. Begin to think of yourself as a spectator – the soul – looking at the human experiences.

My Universal Energies Releasing programme will release you with little effort.

"I love how all big things were being released then other things popped up that were there festering at the back of my mind – released. It absolutely 'wowed' me."

Feedback

We must let go of the fear and guilt relating to someone else's actions, which make you feel this way – let them go!

We need to find our belief and trust. What do you believe, why are you here on Earth, what is your mission, your soul's purpose?

Ask yourself these questions and take some time out to write down your answers.

As soon as you realise your purpose or mission, you will have a glowing perspective on life, and on the things you do; you will stop searching for the proverbial something and will soon realise that what you need will come to you.

Write it! Rip it! Burn it! Flush it!

This is a remarkably successful way of releasing to make way for new things in your life.

Just before I began to write this chapter, someone who works in mental health with autistic children, including some who do not speak, used this method and the child spoke to her after years of not talking.

Self-talk – this is a great way to change your habits – consistently talk yourself into the new you.

Love yourself first. I love myself. There is no ego here, just the pure virgin love we are born with.

Over three decades ago, I retrained in many holistic and business practices. I coached, helped, guided and transformed the lives of many with my short programmes and one-to-one guidance that lead to one's self-realisation.

As a result of working with me, you will have access to my strong intuition and my systems to give you that flow and glow in your life. I will give you a lighter feeling, which is beyond powerful and empowering, bringing drive and determination into your new found thoughts.

You can do whatever you set your mind to, with a little encouragement and accountability.

My life mission and purpose is to be the best version of myself.

To go forward fearlessly in all that I do.

And you can too.

Jan Mayfield

Jan Mayfield is an inspirational speaker and author of *Zoetic Soul: Pertaining to Life. Your Life.* Formerly a teaching and management professional, she switched direction – after experiencing a traumatic accident – to pursue her passion for understanding her soul's purpose in life.

Jan diligently rose from illness and began to release her true self, using a sequence of coordinated events.

For almost three decades, she has been a successful entrepreneur and an intuitive coaching consultant.

Radiating warmth and compassion, this gifted and intuitive woman's unique approach brings insight and empowerment to her clients, offering them the opportunity to reach their souls' full potential.

"I just love how you combine your experience in the personal development industry with your spiritual teachings. The world needs more people like you, especially now."

Landi Jac, Global Director, Worldwide Business Intelligence

www.janmayfield.com

www.universal-energies.com

www.facebook.com/janmayfield11

www.linkedin.com/in/jan-mayfield-10854445/

IWOW
INSPIRATIONAL WOMEN OF THE WORLD

6.
RETRAIN
THE BRAIN

Jenni Dunman

I spend the first 20 years of my life hiding a secret, a horrible secret that I didn't understand or know how to deal with.

My earliest childhood memories are of serious sexual abuse.

Child abuse is not the subject of this story. It is about how you can retrain your brain into removing any negative or traumatic events no matter how deep rooted or heart-breaking.

I spent my childhood keeping this secret, and, coupled with rejection by my father, my young, subconscious mind believed I was loathsome and damaged.

Thinking that this was normal, I didn't know there was any other way to be.

I left home when I was a teenager and started on my path of self-destruction. I had no sense of self-worth and I moved from house-shares to cold bedsits. I had no money, no real friends, no fear.

I put myself into dangerous situations and hung out with very unpleasant people. Watching people fight, take drugs or commit crime didn't scare me. I thought it was where I belonged.

I attracted negative people and negative events into my life, and I had absolutely no goals or ambition. At 19, I lost a baby when I was 20 weeks pregnant. Life became too much to bear and I attempted suicide.

Failing at suicide was the best thing that could ever have happened to me. My first experience of true gratitude.

I'd hit rock bottom and knew I couldn't carry on living my old life. It gave me the hard push I needed to save myself.

My first stop in self-help was the library. The content at that time was limited and there was no internet, but I loved reading so I absorbed everything I found on self-confidence.

I realised through books that I had a natural desire to help people.

I joined the Metropolitan Police when I was 21. I already had a lot of life experience, I was tough and streetwise – plus the post included free food and accommodation, and you got paid while training, so it ticked a lot of boxes for me.

There I learned how to successfully engage with people – from the most disturbing, violent offenders to the most vulnerable victims. I was just naturally good at communicating.

On 7 July 2005, London was hit by terror attacks. I was stationed at Edgware Road and deployed to the scene. It was probably one of a handful of times when I felt scared, but also extremely proud to be there supporting my city.

I remember looking around and seeing so many people from all walks of life showing so much unconditional kindness to strangers. Among the devastation, there was a real feeling of camaraderie. The big, unexpected lesson for me that terrible day was the realisation that most people are actually good and kind.

From this my mindset began improving and I was starting to enjoy life a little. I had bought a small flat and had started dating. My usual pattern of attracting negative men or self-sabotaging with any good ones was a common pattern, so this time I assumed it would be no different.

After 18 months we had bought a new place together. I vividly remember standing in our lovely Victorian flat and asking myself, "Why hasn't he left me yet?"

What happened next, I can only describe as a personal breakthrough because the words that popped into my head, without exaggeration, totally blew my mind.

The words were **"Because you're a nice person."**

It's difficult to explain how completely stunned I was to hear this. I repeated the words over and over in my head for months. Oh my God, I AM a nice person and I deserve to be happy. I couldn't believe that it had taken me until the age of 24 to realise it.

I started reading more books on mindset, law of attraction and psychology. I learned to completely retrain my brain so that all old self-beliefs were completely destroyed.

My life did a complete 180-degree turnaround and it all happened so fast. I began to love myself for the first time and I attracted lifelong friends and let my family back into my life.

I became kinder, more generous and grateful, and I ditched the negative self-talk.

I also married that guy and we have three beautiful children.

When my friend's daughter choked years later, I was there to save her. This led to the launch of Daisy First Aid, a business which teaches parents emergency first aid. This business has been credited in helping save the lives of so many babies and children. As well as winning multiple awards, the business pushed me into the media spotlight as the industry expert and I am a regular guest on TV, radio, stage and online. I have a huge celebrity portfolio, including royalty.

I am now the chief executive of four successful businesses and an investor in ethical startups. I am a global success mindset trainer too, using research undertaken over the last 20 years to show the world that anyone can retrain their brain.

When we are born, we have no anxiety, no insecurities, no fear, no phobias. We have a beautiful clear young mind, ready to be educated.

From the moment we are born, we are influenced by family, friends, school, others' opinions, beliefs, circumstances and events. These things can shape the rest of our lives and can help determine whether we succeed in life or fail.

We don't, however, have to accept that that's just who we are; if your opinion of yourself is negative or you are unhappy, you can retrain your brain.

Any negative self-beliefs will have come from something that happened in your past. This may have been something big and significant, but may have been from something you don't even remember. **Your subconscious mind remembers everything and is your boss.**

So how do you start retraining your brain?

You can start with the words you use.

The words you say out loud and to yourself physically influence your mind and body.

Your brain will believe what you tell it. For example, have you ever pulled a sickie from work, told your manager you were sick and then found yourself actually feeling ill?

It is the reason the placebo pill can cure illnesses.

Start by avoiding any negative, self-sabotaging words. Think about the conversations you have with people. Are they happy, fun, optimistic, glass half full? Or are they moany, shouty, bitchy, mean and negative?

If they are the latter, you absolutely need to reverse this if you want to succeed in living a happy life.

Stop yourself from voicing negative words – change them into a positive. Regardless of the circumstances, there is always something to be grateful for. This may take practice, but I promise that you will instantly start to feel better. Once this practice becomes part of your life, the results will be amazing.

Saying anything negative about anything or anyone will not make you happy.

Instead, be kind to yourself and get used to saying nice things about yourself and everyone around you. Be proud of yourself and celebrate your successes, big and small.

The next thing to consider is who you are spending most of your time with. Do they make you happy when you're around them? Do they make you laugh and smile? Are they your biggest fan? If not, are they enhancing your life for the better or are they hindering your happiness?

These people can have a huge influence on whether you succeed or fail.

You have a choice about the company you keep. If you find yourself feeling drained, sad, angry, irritated or stressed, you should ask yourself how you can best avoid these people. This is your only life, so don't waste it.

Lastly, ask yourself, "Do I have all these positive qualities when I am around others? Do people love spending time with me? Am I a joy to be around? Do I lift their spirits and make people happy?"

You can unknowingly have an impact on the day of hundreds of people just by making one person's day. For example, you tell a stranger that her hair looks beautiful, she feels great and is friendly to a shop assistant, who feels valued and gives great service to her customers, who all leave feeling happy and pass that feeling on to others, creating a big wave of positivity and happiness. Imagine the results of doing this every day.

Jenni Dunman

Jenni Dunman is a multiple award-winning entrepreneur, ethical investor and global mindset transformation coach. She is living proof that you can retrain your brain to overcome any trauma and unhappiness and achieve optimal happiness and life success.

Jenni has dedicated her life to saving lives, physically and mentally, as a former detective sergeant, paediatric first aid expert and coach.

Having suffered extremely traumatic events as a young child, Jenni studied for 20 years, learning how to retrain the negative subconscious mind and how to remove self-sabotaging triggers.

The systems she has created have outstanding results. Jenni has inspired others and changed their lives, using her simple and safe brain retraining techniques.

www.jennidunman.com

INSPIRATIONAL WOMEN OF THE WORLD

7.
FINDING JOY

Joy Whitlock

Introduction

When people say, "Just be yourself" what does it mean? Who am I? I am a mother, daughter, sister, aunt, mother-in-law, friend, employee, boss, business owner, coach – I am an artist, lover and poet. And my name is Joy. So what?

I believe many people don't know who they are and because of that, they waste their lives. They drift along in a monotonous routine, doing what needs to be done each day on the eternal treadmill. I was one of those people. I had developed some harmful traits that I was oblivious to. I had tendencies to self-destruct and a sense that I was never good enough. I had no purpose and little self-worth.

Despite that, I achieved many good things personally and professionally. I grasped opportunities because they were there. It is life-enhancing to work outside your comfort zone, to grow and develop – but without purpose, it is meaningless.

A few years ago, I discovered neurolinguistic programming (NLP) and it transformed my life. I was shocked to discover my unhelpful habits, which had formed in childhood, and amazed at how simple they were to resolve. One profound and emotional day I was coached to discover my life purpose. At the time I had no idea how that hour would affect me. It was a jaw-dropping moment that made me excited for my future. It helped me transform into a better, more effective version of Joy. I feel empowered and in control and I am fulfilling my life purpose. How about you?

Story

As a child I knew I was loved but we didn't show emotions in the family. It was more than the British 'stiff upper lip'. As a little girl, I remember my mild-mannered dad, who wouldn't hurt a fly, smashing a plate on the kitchen floor in anger, and my parents screaming at each other. My brother and I were scared. I learned later that they had vowed after that never to argue in front of the children again. So, I grew up in an emotionally sterile house where the adults didn't love each other or argue. I very quickly learned the art of conflict avoidance and became a child who liked to please, to make Mum happy. These behaviours were useful at the time, but sometimes adversely affected my adult life.

Mum was the driving force. As a young woman, she was spirited and ambitious. She fell in love with a man of colour, which was strictly taboo in the 1950s. Her father did his best to destroy the relationship and she was married off to an older man, to make her conform. She became a suppressed and depressed 60s housewife and took barbiturates for years. Her spirit was destroyed. Mum was determined that my brother and I would not waste our lives as she felt she had.

The truth is that we rarely fulfil our potential because we don't know what it is or how to achieve it. I inherited Mum's spirit. I was always striving for more, but I didn't know why.

I went to St Bartholomew's Hospital School of Nursing, one of the most famous teaching hospitals in the world, to do my training. A prodigious career commenced, perfect for a people pleaser. Nursing is an incredible yet challenging career. It was not all frilly hats, starched aprons and flirting with doctors. (The uniform I wore as a student nurse is in a museum – I'm mortified!) It is a tough but rewarding job.

We do personal and intimate things to people. We see babies born into this world and care for people as they leave. We laugh one minute and cry the next. Gone were the emotionless days of youth.

A curious and privileged career was under way. I pushed professional boundaries and became one of the early practice nurses. I worked with some progressive GPs. We were among the first to set up nurse-led clinics and a surgery. I remember one patient who lived a slightly breathless, wheezy life. I changed his inhalers and a year later he came to see me. He told me that he was fitter than he could ever remember and was training for a marathon. This was one of those magic moments where you know you have made a real difference.

I fell in love, married and had two wonderful sons. Yet I was constantly restless. Searching for something, but I didn't know what. I didn't know how to discuss emotions and avoided conflict. I ruined a good relationship.

One problem with being a people pleaser was that I found myself doing things I didn't really want to do, the jobs that everyone else had managed to avoid. Why couldn't I say, "No," like everyone else?

My second long-term relationship turned out to be toxic. I unwittingly allowed myself to be manipulated over food and relationships. He would leave the food I had lovingly prepared and accuse me of giving him rubbish. So, what did I do? I would scurry round and cook something different to please him. He tried to isolate me and stop me seeing my sons and friends by causing conflict and making me choose between him and them. The butterflies of excitement slowly turned to stomach-churning fear. It was insidious, as these things so often are. I waited for my moment. When he threatened to leave again, instead of begging him to stay, to avoid conflict and trying to please (see how repetitive these are), I helped him out the door. How did a strong person like me become a victim? I can answer that now.

A colleague trained in NLP and developed an introductory course. I went along out of curiosity. I learned more about the art of communication and defining goals. I was starting to think about myself and what I wanted in life. Those two days were incredible. I was blown away by the powerful impact and wanted to learn more. Over the following three years I became a master practitioner and trainer.

One day we learned about Robert Dilts' neurological levels. The top level is your life purpose. I remember sitting there thinking I hadn't a clue, and then it struck me like a bolt of lightning. My purpose was to make a difference to others. Was it really that simple? I had been doing that all my life without realising. I burst into tears as this knowledge sank in. It was the difference that made a difference. I felt elated.

Having purpose enabled me to redefine my identity and beliefs and values. Knowing what was important reinforced my decision-making. It gave me permission to stop doing the things that added no value or didn't support my purpose. I could finally say, "No." I know I'm now making an invaluable difference to others in a meaningful way.

There is a technique called timeline therapy. I walked back to the first memory of when my superb inability to deal with conflict developed. Yes, you guessed it – back to the plate throwing and screaming event. I was coached to change my experience of it and to receive the resources to deal with conflict in the future. No more sweeping things under the carpet and pretending things are fine when they aren't.

Two sayings often come to mind. "If you don't value yourself, how do you expect others to?" And, "Whether you think you can, or you think you can't – you're right," (attributed to Henry Ford). It is a self-fulfilling prophesy.

I grew up believing I was rubbish at art. The only drawings I did were anatomical, for professional exams. I quite fancied throwing paint at a canvas, like Jackson Pollock. I used an NLP technique to experience what it may be like to be an artist. The overwhelming messages I got from standing in artists' shoes (YouTube is a wonderful thing) were to enjoy the creative process and not worry about the result. Eagerly, I cycled to the nearest arts and craft store. I came back with two bags containing things to get me started swinging from my handlebars. I absolutely loved the creative experience and was quite pleased with my first abstract. An accountant wanted to buy one of my paintings. He asked me how much. I said £1,000 and he bartered and bought it for £700. Since then, I have sold quite a few paintings because I believed I could and valued myself.

I have finally found Joy – the purposeful, ambitious, determined and creative version that is loving life and making a difference in the world. NLP helped me change my life in so many ways and it will yours too if you so choose.

The most profound thing you can do is to identify your purpose in life. This may change over time and that is OK. Once you have purpose, everything else falls into place. Your identity and beliefs and values will align to your purpose. Understand them and write them down. Review them regularly and amend them as you see fit.

One last thought. We get more of what we focus on. It doesn't matter if it is positive or negative. Deal with the negative and focus on the things that are important. You have the capability to be the best version of yourself. Know you are amazing and fulfil your life purpose.

Much love

Joy

Joy Whitlock

Joy is an international trainer and presenter who is dedicated to making a difference to others. She is a skilled facilitator and mediator.

She has had a long, highly successful and varied career in healthcare. The discovery of NLP helped to change her life. She is now an NLP master practitioner and trainer and an executive coach with a diploma in applied positive psychology.

Joy excels at working with individuals and teams to become the best they can in their professional and personal lives. She has worked with world champions and chief executives, and has helped people who considered themselves to be ordinary to become extraordinary versions of themselves. She is here to make a difference to you, whoever you are and whatever you want to achieve.

www.joywhitlock.co.uk

IWOW
INSPIRATIONAL WOMEN OF THE WORLD

8.
NATURE'S GIFT

Karen Ramsay-Smith

As I walked around the lake, a sensation of overwhelming emotion rose from deep within my stomach, through my chest and up into my throat: a terrible, aching pain, desperate to be released. I held on to it for a moment, a little embarrassed by my tears. I touched the petals of a rose, by the hedgerow, listening to the cry of a buzzard above me. I could smell the lake, and my breathing felt shallow as I struggled to hold back the tears. It was then that I heard a voice, saying, "Let go, feel this grief, he is here; these tears are just love and it is OK to love, it's OK not to be OK. I love you."

Wonderful memories flooded my mind and my heart swelled open as more tears came, leaking on to my cheeks as I blinked and let them run like a river. I missed him, but I knew he was there with me and I was grateful for my life and his. "Thank you," I said, "thank you for these moments we shared together." I breathed in a little deeper this time, knowing I had this space. Being out in nature had helped me once before, and I knew it would help me get through this again. I paused and looked at the sky for what seemed like several minutes. I watched a cloud as it morphed and changed. I knew that I was somehow connected with him and he was connected with me, and I felt my emotions ease. My body became less heavy and I had an incredible sense of peace as I walked home.

Back in September 2019, I was still in the process of accepting the sudden loss of my mum in March from a brain tumour. I was dealing with probate, because my dad had died 10 years previously, also from a brain tumour. I was running the family home and my business as a coach and mentor too, when shockingly, out of the blue, my partner went missing after we had separated earlier that month.

I waited anxiously by the phone for the police search for him to be positively concluded, but I knew deep in my gut that something was terribly wrong. As a practising mindfulness teacher and coach, I had spent many hours working on my ability to remain present and balanced at times of emotional challenge. Being connected with myself in this way, I sensed that my partner of 11 years was very separated from me on those few days. I felt it in my body, but had no idea that I was about to be told he had just taken his own life.

I began to realise that the awful separation I sensed was not anxiety, but grief. The phone rang and in an instant my life changed forever. His body was found in a beautiful place of nature: Hope Wood in Somerset.

My partner, Daz, had a huge, beautiful beard. To most who knew him, he was an outgoing, happy-go-lucky guy who loved to look good and listened to all kinds of music. He even took a speaker into the bathroom when going to shower. He was always busy taking selfies for his Instagram feed, was very connected online and had a large network of friends in the bearding community.

As his partner, I saw a different side to him. Although I knew little of how severely he suffered with his thoughts, over the years I noticed his growing difficulty in staying still, his need for constant distraction, and his struggle to be alone.

Outwardly, he looked like a confident, fun, mentally and physically strong man who enjoyed his job and his life. Inwardly, however, he struggled to express his emotions. He told me that he didn't care what others thought, but I could tell he did. He felt bullied in his adult life and that he'd been pushed out of groups since childhood; he was seeking validation and struggled to take responsibility for his own choices.

We loved to walk our puppy, Harry, in quiet places of nature. Despite his need for constant distractions, when Daz was out in the natural world, he found peace. It had a calming effect on him. He enjoyed listening to and watching wildlife – it was a place where he told me he had sought sanctuary since he was a little boy, but he rarely gave himself the time to access it as an adult. We shared a deep love of nature together.

During the weeks following his death, along with his family and friends, we raised almost £6k for his funeral and funds for a charity close to those in the bearding world. The Lions Barber Collective is an international collection of top barbers who have come together to raise awareness of mental health for the prevention of suicide. Not long afterwards, I began a campaign and a community to support mental health awareness, called #loveYOUmore and I am coaching and mentoring again.

Losing my partner in this devastating way, on top of the loss of both my parents and my own breakdown over the last 10 years, made this the most challenging and transformational period of my life. To most, this appears to be a series of devastating events. However, I remained incredibly resilient and balanced.

I have been told many times how strong I am. I've been asked how I could continue to help others while this was going on. The answer is simple. I have a practice of being present with myself. I have learned to listen and be present through personal and professional challenges. I regularly practise meditation, allowing myself to feel my emotions and letting my thoughts come and go. This helps me to trust myself and respond to life in a more balanced way.

So many of us rush through our lives, anxious and frustrated about tomorrow or stuck in the past. Where are we going? How do we get there? Our entire existence is experienced in our mind, constantly pushing our emotions to one side to answer the call of another expectation. We believe that we can 'think' our way to a better place: a better job, house, holiday – a better life. We live our lives through our thoughts, and our habits of distraction from our emotions keep us stuck. We live lives that feel as though no matter how much we 'do', we continue to feel separated, disconnected and unfulfilled.

I strongly believe we do not have to live this way. We all have our own personal coach within us. A natural born state, completely free for us to access at any time. Nature is one of the best ways to meet this inner teacher. When I run my mindful coaching retreats, there is access to nature for the simple reason that being present with yourself this way is an incredibly powerful experience; it unlocks a state of being that provides the foundation for a peaceful, balanced and more fulfilled life.

When we are always talking and doing, we are never listening. We must learn to listen and let go if we want to create more of what we really want, learning to observe our fearful self, to master our flow of thoughts and emotions.

Being in a natural flow this way helps those I support to achieve a balance between 'being' and 'doing'. If we strive to suffer less, we must accept that separation and grief are as much a part of life as happiness and joy. The reason we suffer so much is that we are separated from our own sense of our spirit: our true natural self. Ultimately, we must learn to let go and feel every emotion – good and bad.

When was the last time you created space to be quiet and just listen? There is something inside you that is always asking you to stop and listen. Natural connection with yourself in this way will bring you a sense of freedom and clarity in your mind, ease in your body, and unconditional love into your life.

My purpose is to support you to remember your true natural self, to create your life on a foundation of inner balance, resilience and peace through compassion, self-awareness and personal mastery.

Our natural world is ready to support you to open up to all of this. I am excited and inspired to create more nature retreats and programmes that will support many more women to remember the truth of who they are. This is nature's gift.

"Karen is a highly intuitive and compassionate coach. She is incredibly skilled at picking up what issues need particular focus at the different points along the coaching journey. Karen has guided me to a place of better self-awareness and her coaching has been transformational for both my work and personal life. Karen has brought me greater self-awareness and presence in the moment. She has equipped me with techniques and strategies to cope with different situations, giving me a toolkit for a better life."

Joyce

Karen Ramsay-Smith

Karen is a professional advanced transformational coach, accredited by the Association for Coaching, and a mindfulness teacher, accredited by Mindfulness CIC. She combines deep transformational coaching approaches, mindfulness tools and techniques, supporting clients to generate clarity, vision and purpose in their lives, creating lasting transformational change.

Before setting up her coaching business, Bigger Picture Coaching, Karen spent 25 years in marketing and communications, the latter in a senior strategic capacity.

Karen's mindful approach to life has helped her to grow through personal and professional challenges. Her coaching practice has enabled her to serve her clients and networks powerfully. She coaches and mentors private individuals and corporate groups to form deeper relationships with themselves and the natural world, hosting events and mindful retreats with speaking and meditation guidance. She has been featured in online interviews and published books, and on the radio. Her coaching has been described as compassionate and life-changing.

www.biggerpicturecoaching.com

INSPIRATIONAL WOMEN OF THE WORLD

9.
CONNECTING AGAIN

Kerry Martin

Ever since I was a child, I always knew I wanted to be a leader. I've always felt connected within myself and I've always been at my happiest when I'm around people. I love the process of meeting, connecting and building relationships with others. I truly believe in the value of human connection and I attribute a lot of my success to it.

Some events that started in 2014 saw me lose that connection, to myself, to others and to the world. It would take me nearly five years to heal, rebuild and feel connected again.

I was born in Luton, 44 years ago, prematurely. I couldn't wait to come into the world. I had an amazing childhood, raised in a secure home that was full of love, care and happiness. When my older sister and I were growing up, we never wanted for anything and my parents made a lot of sacrifices to give us that. They shaped the person I have become today, and I will be grateful to them forever.

From a young age, I knew I was going to be a leader. I would dream of leading, being on stage and teaching others. My mum would catch me in my room, standing up, talking to all my dolls and teddies, which I had lined up in rows on the floor. I'd be in my fantasy world, pretending to be their leader. Even the doll rivals, Barbie and Sindy, were made to be friends. It is a vision that has been realised many times throughout my career, being on stage, teaching, leading others and encouraging them to cheer each other on. Even the Barbie and Sindy dolls of my real-life teams made the transition into liking and supporting each other.

After being bullied in junior school by a girl in my class, I wanted to be a leader, so that I could create the environment I worked in. A dinner lady showed me compassion and kindness and I still remember today how that made me feel. I wanted to be that leader who held people's hands in their time of need.

I started working for a retailer and in 2000 became one of its leaders. In my 17-year career with the company, I worked my way up to regional management. I loved my role with a passion. I invested a lot of my time in mentoring and coaching my teams. When I spotted talent in people, it seemed that they didn't believe in their potential. It was my role to coach and nurture them. I led with the philosophy that if I looked after my people, they would look after me. I served them and believed in leading with love and compassion. I was criticised heavily for it, being called too sensitive, pink and fluffy by some of my leaders and peers. I knew that by showing your teams you cared, you would break down the barriers that stand between management and colleagues, as long as you had boundaries. I created open and honest working environments and I built teams that cheered each other on. I made a consistent effort to get to know as many people as I could, building strong relationships. As a result, we had a lot of success over the years and won several awards.

Like most successful leaders, I had my fair share of standing down bullies over the years and there were those who attempted to destroy my reputation. Retail teaches you to have a thick skin, so I let a lot of it bounce off me, carried on smiling and got on with my job.

My life was turned upside down in 2014, the most difficult year of my life. I found myself dealing with different situations that all occurred at the same time. My life became difficult at work, with a new leader, and out of work, with a female friend. I was dealing with emotional abuse from her consistently, having been on a weight loss journey. This caused me to suffer from anxiety for the first time in my life. It was very new for me and I didn't know how to deal with it. After years of being happy and fulfilled, something died inside me and my family noticed the changes in me.

After 17 years of commitment, hard work and loyalty, I parted ways with the business and it broke my heart. I walked away from all situations that caused my wellbeing to suffer. I missed my training and trainer. I loved both, but things had become strained there as well because of everything. The damage had been done and it would be a long road ahead. I had lost everything. My confidence had been shattered, my self-respect had gone, and I felt worthless. Every day was a constant struggle and I found it difficult to function. I lost connection with myself and my friends, and I no longer had the connections at work. I had my family and three friends who helped me through it all.

The one positive thing to come out of it was spending quality time with my mum. That is something money cannot buy, and we connected more and more each day.

The next year bought more pain and grief: I lost my mum to sepsis.

Her death crushed me and I just didn't know how I would cope without her. I was swamped in grief and turned to emotional eating. A year later, I was then faced with a health issue after finding a lump on my breast. I made a deal with myself: I would get my life back on track if I could just come through it. I was lucky and did. It was the kick that I needed.

I decided to sign up for a trek in China to support a sepsis charity, which had supported me in my grief and loss – I wanted to give back. This was a big turning point for me. I met an amazing group of people and, for the first time in a long time, I started to feel alive again. I could be myself around this group and they accepted me for who I was.

I had spent the previous four years studying and had coaching qualifications. I wasn't doing anything with them, because of my mindset. I started looking at how I could help myself; this is when personal development and mindfulness were introduced into my life. These were the game changers that really transformed my life. This year, I qualified as a mindfulness practitioner.

Mindfulness taught me to leave the past behind and let go of everything. I forgave those who hurt me and I forgave myself for my reactions and behaviour. I let go of the guilt I had held on to for so long. I mentally told myself to move on with my life and stop standing still. It helped me find the leader within myself again and reignite my zest for life. I learned to focus on the present and be present.

Personal development helped me to believe in myself, love myself and regain my confidence again. It was a magical journey and I became part of a community that supported me. It reminded me that I could do anything I wanted to do, and I could create the life I wanted.

I am now the proud owner of my own coaching business and I help people by coaching them in **leadership, which** shaped who I am; **mindfulness, which** saved me; and **personal development, which** taught me to believe in myself again. I have created a community for people to feel supported, so that we can help each other – something that I wish I'd had access to back in 2014.

For the first time in six years, I feel connected again to myself, others and the world. Anxiety is a thing of the past and I am happy. It seems so perfect to be able to combine my professional and personal experience with my qualifications to help others.

When I was moving home I found a box full of thank you letters and cards from ex-colleagues; one said, "Thank you for treating me like a human being."

I met a store manager who told me that the team still talked about me after all these years. It made me realise just how much impact I'd had on other people.

The art of connection is becoming lost in the ever-changing world of technology. If there is one message I could spread to everyone on this planet, it would be keep the art of human connection alive, show up, be present and make everyone you meet feel valued. Hold someone's hand and help them through life, and don't forget to smile.

Kerry Martin

Kerry Martin is an experienced coach who specialises in the field of personal development, leadership and mindfulness. She excels in building successful teams, communities and culture. She has a passion for opening her client's minds to new and productive ways of thinking, building up their confidence in the process to reach their full potential.

Kerry has 20 years' experience in leading teams at a senior level. She led teams to perform at the highest level, helping develop top performers, coaches and centre of excellence trainers.

Kerry will take you on the magical journey of personal development, helping you to bridge the gap from where you are to where you want to be. Her mission is to keep the art of human connection alive. A great attribute is her ability to connect and share on a deep level of consciousness. She creates safe environments for her clients to grow in both their personal and professional lives.

www.kerrymartincoaching.com

INSPIRATIONAL WOMEN OF THE WORLD

10.
MY LIFE MASK-FREE

LaChelle Adkins

As a pastor's wife, mother of 15, community volunteer and entrepreneur, I have learned that women struggle with the desire to please others. They strive for perfection and sacrifice their desires to meet the needs of their family and children. We often preach the importance of self-care, but we live life behind the mask of unfulfillment and sadness. I believed that hiding behind masks would allow me to be successful and be all things to all people. However, I found that it left me powerless, unhappy and seeking validation from others. I am now passionate about shattering those realities and empowering women to determine their own standards, change their mindsets and live their lives to the fullest without limits.

How does one have a 'normal' life after three stays in hospital due to stress and depression? "Am I ever going to get it right? Will I ever be able to build a healthy relationship with my children after being in a behavioural hospital?" These were just some of the questions I asked myself after my third hospital stay. How would I be able to align my values and beliefs with such a dark past? I began to realise that the life I was living did not match the person that I knew myself to be. How could I use this story of victimhood and defeat and turn it into something that I could be proud of and share with my children and other women who may have struggled with the same situation?

After many internal dialogues, based on many questions, I believed that I could sum up how I overcame this situation in five steps:

1. Awareness

2. Personal accountability

3. Change begins with me

4. Self-knowledge

5. Sharing my story with others.

What does a 'normal' life look like and would I be able to maintain it once I achieved it?

Step one involved awareness of the things I had allowed, and caused me to spiral down a road that left me powerless and out of control. I realised that I was a product of my past decisions, which are permanent and cannot be changed. I examined that past and agonised over it, because I believed it did not represent the person that I was.

I thought about my future and the legacy that I wanted to leave for my children – a powerless victim was far from the image that I wanted to have. As I examined my pattern of three hospitalisations, I believed that the odds would be against me if I did not intentionally make a change to prevent this cycle from recurring for a fourth time.

I examined my triggers and patterns and separated my reality from my fairy tale. I was able to observe my behaviour because the outcomes had already occurred. I asked myself the hard questions about why I'd acted in that manner, which had resulted in the life that I was currently living. If I was a successful high achiever, then why was my life not reflecting that reality?

This led to step two – personal accountability for my actions. I realised that blame, bitterness and resentment did not serve me, no matter how much I believed that I was right, and others were wrong. I learned that I had no power in blaming people, places and things for what happened to me. I was raised to be a winner and a high achiever, one who finds a way to solve a problem rather than an excuse.

It was at that point that I realised that I didn't recognise the person that I saw reflecting back at me in the mirror. I had lost the person who had begun my journey of parenthood and marriage. Somehow, we had become separated, as my family grew, along with all the responsibilities and what I believed were family and marriage goals.

As I anxiously awaited the fruits of my labour, they were often buried beneath more delayed promises that were second to ministry, military advancements, community service, career promotions, and high expectations for academically stellar children. These were all things that I aspired to have, but the problem was that I believed that I had to sacrifice my happiness and fulfilment in the process. How could this supermom, who was highly engaged in her children's spiritual, physical, emotional, and academic life, not have the ability to advocate for her needs as a wife and mother?

The story that played in my head was that it was not that serious. I would just be a little delayed and how could I be selfish to ask for anything when my husband was working around the clock to make ends meet? I just needed to continue to pick up the slack and keep working harder until a breakthrough came.

After my last stay in hospital, I realised that the compliments from strangers and people outside my home were fleeting seconds of happiness and may be retracted if they saw how much laundry was in my laundry room, how many dishes were in my sink, and that my children, who were stellar at school, had unmade beds at home.

I could clearly see at this point that I was placing my power and happiness in the hands of others, based on the criteria they chose to use to gauge my success. I would hear compliments daily from teachers, family, friends and strangers – they would all be cancelled when I hit the door of defeat as I walked into my own home. I no longer wanted to ride the roller coaster of emotions with no control. I chose to reconnect with the person I'd lost 13 years ago. I decided to gather all those lemons amassed over the course of 13 years and create my own lemonade stand.

Now we are at step three and this is the point of change. I had to transform all these lemons into the lemonade. The challenge was even greater when I realised that the lemons were me. I was the only catalyst that I had the power to change. I recalled that hospital visit number three was the result of depending on others, as well as myself, to change. When new patterns appeared to not work, the path of least resistance was to revert to the comfort zone of what was familiar.

As I'd observed from my two previous stays in hospital, only I could be responsible for me and I needed to be the change agent in my new story. This is where I learned the meaning of empathy and compassion. I was able to see my past and take the hardest step and forgive myself for the actions that I had and had not taken. I had to stand up and put to rest all the shoulds, woulds, and coulds surrounding a story that I chose not to make real. If my version of the story that I created was not real, then maybe all the judgments that I'd made about others were not real.

It was then that I chose to let go of what was false and grab on to what was real and work on creating a life of happiness and gratitude. Forgiveness was the ingredient that led to my change, where I was self-fulfilled, able to see my flaws and love myself unconditionally without seeking validation from others.

Who did I want to be in my story and what steps was I determined to take to accomplish it? Here is the transformation of those lemons, which created a new foundation to build a timeless masterpiece. I cut my hair, stopped watching television, paused social media, worked part-time as a waitress and hired a business coach. All this was a journey to rekindle the fire that had dimmed in a part of my life. I was raised as a high achiever and I longed to include that part to my story so that I would be complete and ready to tackle the world without the error of believing that my worth was attached to the roles that I chose.

That transformation was the final step that groomed me to teach other women how to do the same thing in their lives. My own journey helped me to expose my fears and sadness with transparency, which led me to create my own FRESH start philosophy. My story created a platform to connect with others and present a safe environment in which to coach women through their own transformation. This journey has allowed me to create new boundaries, systems and relationships, which have transcended my vision way beyond a lemonade stand.

LaChelle Adkins

LaChelle Adkins, 'America's SuperMom', has the ability to juggle career, marriage and 15 children with a smile instead of stress.

She is a lifestyle designer who assists in the transformation of her clients from stress, anxiety and people-pleasing to confidence, boundaries and happiness. She accomplishes this through her podcast, inspirational speaking and coaching programme – which covers her FRESH start philosophy – and her YouTube videos. She is passionate about educating others about the importance of mental wellness, after her own 13-year battle with depression and three hospital stays.

During the global pandemic of 2020, she created a #smile4wellness movement to empower others to be proactive with mental health. SMILE – sleep, mood, inner voice, laughter and energy – are key pillars to help maintain wellness if monitored and adjusted daily as necessary.

She and her husband of 27 years, Jerome, live outside Atlanta with 10 of their 15 children.

www.lachelleadkins.com

11.
THE TRUTH OF IT

Leanne Eustace

Running a business can often be hard, frustrating, lonely and tiring. It is not for everyone and it can bring an unbelievable level of stress and responsibility. It took me a long time to realise that you can't do everything yourself.

I run a successful business, manage a fantastic team, work closely with a range of clients and maintain a competitive edge using systems and technology to maintain control and improve efficiencies.

I still have the time, focus and positive energies to be a happy mum, cook meals, run the household, handle the chores and enjoy precious me-time.

My career can be summarised as milestones, each one a crossroads in my life. I'm a great believer that everything happens for a reason and live my life with a work hard, play hard philosophy.

Thinking back to my school days, I was devasted to have my grades based mainly on coursework, on account of having been in hospital with suspected meningitis. Luckily, I had put in an immense amount of effort and on this occasion (as academic study never seems to come easy to me), it taught me to always try my best.

At 16, I moved to Somerset with Lee (yes – my husband), suddenly needing to earn money and realising what's involved running a house.

As a waitress doing shift work and relying on public transport, I wished I could achieve more, so I became a marketing assistant. I thought I had found the dream job.

When I arrived at work one morning the accounts department was short-staffed, and I, as the youngest employee, was assigned to the team. I won't lie, I was devastated and hated the thought. Astonishingly, I fell in love with accounting and found my true vocation.

Unable to afford the qualifications, but determined, I searched for a way to become a chartered accountant. I discovered that government-funded training was available for someone living in Wales and working in accounts.

With my training options agreed, I moved to Cardiff and embarked on finding an employer. One recruitment agent warned me that "as an unqualified, pretty, young lady" I would "not get very far in the industry".

My ambitions were now focused – I was going to become a financial controller for a multi-million-pound-turnover business.

Somehow, being told, "You're not going to achieve your dreams" made me more determined to demonstrate my capabilities. One should never judge a book by its cover.

Having secured a job as a purchase ledger clerk, I embarked on my journey, working full-time while studying in the evening and at weekends for an AAT (Association of Accounting Technicians) degree-level accounting qualification.

I was ecstatic on completion; I had a degree. To celebrate, I was given my very first Cross pen. I love stationery, so it is a treasured gift, reminding me of my experiences. It is still my lucky pen, which I use every day.

Determined to develop, I became an accounts assistant. I learned a great deal in industry and began the ACCA (Association of Chartered Certified Accountants) qualification in my own time. Studying for chartered level while working full-time was tough.

Challenging myself and learning to set goals with time frames meant achieving milestones and I progressed to be the management accountant in a large organisation, but I was on a mission to become a financial controller.

I did it. Despite not being ACCA qualified, my determination, personality and work experience helped me secure a position as financial controller for a large international business.

Feeling on top of the world, happily and successfully heading a team, reporting directly to the board of directors, I was living the dream, but lost my spirit. Once I had learned the job and the team and systems were running efficiently, my role was merely reporting. Valid suggestions I made were ignored, as the company was already profitable.

This infuriated me. Numbers help businesses, by allowing trends to be spotted, resulting in more accurate budgeting and planning and, most importantly, goals being achieved.

Several people told me I did not match the 'normal' personality profile of an accountant. I was never quite sure whether this was meant as a compliment or criticism, but it resonated with me. I'd never fitted in with classmates, having a different background from them, and I was not afraid to ask questions or share answers and opinions.

Being approached with an opportunity to teach the AAT qualification was overwhelming. Although I'd never thought of it, I relished the opportunity. It's amazing how accounts are right or wrong, yet you can explain the calculation methods in various ways.

Friends continually asked me to explain accounting. I would question why they needed this, having already appointed an accountant. I was bemused to hear answers such as, "Don't want to feel stupid," and "Don't want to pay for more time," and my all-time favourite, "I don't understand how it helps me."

The accounting industry is about so much more than the legal red tape it's known for. With good accountants, financial information is like magic – saving time and money and helping achieve goals.

Everything pointed to setting up a practice and I didn't want to have the 'what-if' scenario on my conscience, so we started our business, Accounted For.

For nearly 15 years, I have been a successful businesswoman, helping thousands of business owners. Empowering you to follow your dreams and do what you love each day would be my ultimate success story.

Entrepreneurs are familiar with phrases such as, 'Knowledge is power,' 'Cash is king,' and 'Turnover is vanity; profit is sanity,' but I believe that time is the most important thing – you can never get it back.

These are my tips about how you should spend your valuable time, to reach your potential. They are based on my experience over the years, and no matter where you are on your business journey, these are always worth reviewing:

- Personal goals – set these out and be specific. Know what you want to achieve.

- Business goals – use your personal ones to help create them – that's why you're doing it. Again, be specific.

- Structure – ensure that you use the most appropriate and tax-efficient legal structure for your business.

- Emotion – connect to your goals, build your values, define your company ethos.

- Plan – if you don't already have one, create a business plan outlining how you can achieve your goals.

- Budget – turn your plan into a budget with numbers, values and time frames in line with the planning, and don't forget equipment purchases or expansion plans.

- Cashflow – create a cashflow forecast to analyse whether you could encounter any issues, make additional investments, or plan timings well to save tax.

- Professional advice – engaging help with the financials is beneficial even at planning stage. You would be surprised at the advice available and the efficiencies that can be made.

- Evaluate – compare the plans to your actual results each month, being honest. You are kidding yourself if you adjust the plans, but this doesn't mean that they can't evolve.

- Technology – use it! Review your business operational procedures and check that they are efficient and make the best use of automation.

- Real-time data – create an accounting system with data that's readily available and accurate, so that you can quickly make educated business decisions.

- Business decisions – understand the effect these can have on your business and assess the potential impact before being hasty, but move swiftly to gain a competitive advantage.

- People – know your strengths and weaknesses, and those of other people – use them to full advantage.

- Internal communication – regular team meetings are critical to everyone feeling part of the team, understanding the goals of the business and individuals, and encouraging success.

- External communication – stay in touch with all your stakeholders. People know only the information that has been shared with them.

- Behaviour – exude your company values and ethos in your attitude. We are a family business and I always try to adhere to a system of 'treating others how I want to be treated'.

- Exit strategy – what do you want to achieve ultimately and how and when do you intend to exit the business?

- Protection — you need to ensure that your wills, power of attorney documents and insurances are in place, appropriate and up to date.

We have witnessed and are honoured to have been involved in many success stories including (but not limited to):

- Startup business selling for millions

- Turning over first million

- Paying off home mortgage

The most successful businesses that we see outsource their accounting function and when appropriate use us in the capacity of a finance director, ensuring:

- that a complete system review is conducted

- that the business owner is not left with a day-to-day responsibility, so they can spend their time how they want, playing to their strengths

- the regular production of management accounts: comparing budgeted to expected results and highlighting areas to focus on.

Therefore, I would actively encourage you to engage a good accountant who should be able to save you money and time and add value to your business in ways you may not have thought possible.

A client in construction once told me that although they had had an accountant for years, they had no system, so only knew when their house had burnt down. Now, with the new system, they not only know that their house is on fire, but also which room to look at to put it out.

In summary, have faith, believe that you can have it all and believe in yourself; you can achieve anything.

Leanne Eustace

Leanne Eustace is an expert in accountancy and business. She is known for her passion and enthusiasm as an entrepreneur, chartered accountant, finance tutor, Sage advisory board member and business owner, with over 20 years' experience in a range of sectors and extensive knowledge of tax, planning and structures.

Leanne is an extremely motivated and determined woman on a mission to empower and inspire others to follow their dreams. She is perfectly positioned to demonstrate that understanding and planning your numbers is fundamental to being successful in business, using honest, transparent and relevant skills to help others achieve their goals.

Leanne has strong multitasking capabilities, professionally and personally. As a wife and mum to four boys and two dogs, she tackles washing mountains and toy tornados. She conducts herself with compassion and empathy, and is known as a happy, positive, fun, beach-loving appreciator of gin and cocktails and collector of shoes.

www.accountedforltd.co.uk

www.facebook.com/Accountedforltd

www.linkedin.com/in/leanne-eustace-AFL

INSPIRATIONAL WOMEN OF THE WORLD

12.
LIFE IS FOR LIVING

Lynsey Anne Toft

It's never too late and you're never too old to have a Plan B or start your life again. The only time that it is too late is when the 'shit hits the fan' and you've got no way out. However, don't wait until this happens to regain control of your life. We are living in a time where opportunities are everywhere. You were born to live a life that you truly deserve. The time is now. You can make it happen.

As a little girl I had big dreams. I wanted to be an astronaut, but was told that because I had bad eyes it would never happen. I wanted to live in a big house like the kind you see on TV, but was told that money doesn't make you happy, and that "it doesn't grow on trees" – along with all the other dream-crushing beliefs that end up being instilled in most of us throughout our lives. Every time I dared to dream big, I would quickly be brought down to earth with a bang and told that life isn't a fairy tale and that I needed to get in the real world.

I grew up in a deprived area with working class grandparents. They pushed me to be academic and to study and go to university as a way out of the poverty that they had faced. To achieve this, they wanted me to get a good 'sensible' job, study hard and pass my exams; they felt like this would set me up for life. I'm sure that their intentions were good and that they didn't aim to crush my dreams or give me a poor money mindset. They simply wanted what was best for me and didn't know any different.

So, I did what I had been prepped to do: I got my degree and went on to study to become a teacher. It's crazy how much influence your parents have on your life, by grooming you into a way of life that they want for you. I was conforming to the role perfectly.

I taught in colleges for a short period, but quickly found my passion in the offender learning sector.

I went on to become a teacher in the Prison Service and absolutely loved it. I felt that I was genuinely helping people. I was teaching adults who wanted to learn. I would also help grandparents read so that they could read the letters from their grandchildren, as well as other wonderful things. It was really rewarding and I felt that I was making a difference. I really thought that I had found my calling.

I worked hard, got home late, took work home with me and didn't question it, as I believed this to be the norm. After all, wishing your life away, counting down the hours to the end of the day, weekends and school holidays was what life was like for most people.

Then one day this all changed. I had my first child and nearly died in the process. I was ill for a very long time afterwards, but continued to battle and struggle for years to come. On top of this, my husband was made redundant and we were in trouble. We'd gone from having two good jobs, to suddenly having only one maternity wage coming in. On top of this, my husband had to stay home to look after me, instead of going back to work. We couldn't afford to pay our bills, we racked up a load of debt and had even resorted to selling furniture to survive. I had hit rock bottom and was desperate for a way out.

At that time, a good friend of mine, having witnessed the state of me, recommended that I read *The Secret* by Rhonda Byrne. I thought he was crazy as it sounded so far-fetched, but I figured that I had nothing to lose. I read the book and was determined to give it a go. I wrote my letter to the universe, which included having my own business, working from home to take care of my children, having money and so on. I also put cheques around my house and started to imagine my new life with all this money coming my way. Weirdly, little things did start happening. At first, I thought they were a coincidence, but the coincidences kept happening, so I was sold. This was genuine.

With our newly adopted abundance mindset, we made the decision to move back to Wales. Houses were cheaper and living costs lower there, so we could afford to survive and hopefully have less financial strain, which would allow us to look at other business ideas. I handed in my notice and found a tenant for my house, with no job or house to move to, trusting that the universe would work it out for me, based on my newfound faith.

I found a job, which I subsequently lost due to ill health. I was still struggling after losing so much blood, and my immune system was weak. I ended up having to take a lot of sick leave, after catching all the illnesses the children were picking up at nursery school. This was really tough and I cried for a day, as we had no other income coming in, but then pulled myself together and decided to put my 'big girl pants' on. I had 28 days, while I was still being paid, to figure something else out.

This taught me an invaluable lesson. Employers don't really care about you. To them you are just a number and are totally dispensable. You put them first, resulting in missing out on important milestones, such as school plays, then end up becoming overworked and stressed out. Whereas, if you suddenly died, they would replace you in an instant. I vowed never to put myself in the same position again, where my life was in someone else's hands.

I had realised that life was too short to just pay bills and die. When I complained that life was like Groundhog Day, friends who were also parents would just say, "That's life."

"Well," I thought, "this is not what I want my life to be." I had come close to losing it once and I was determined to change things, once and for all.

So there I was, skint, jobless and in debt, but with a burning desire this time to change it. However, with hindsight, I am grateful that all of this happened, because without it, I would have remained comfortable, and wouldn't have been desperate enough to take such drastic action. Because let's face it, nothing exciting ever happens in your comfort zone.

I had always wanted to get into property investment, but thought that you needed money to do this. This quickly changed, however, after a friend introduced me to *Rich Dad, Poor Dad*. This book, by Robert Koyasaki, was a total revelation to me, and I quickly realised that I had experienced the 'poor dad' while growing up, which was going to require a serious mindset shift on my part. Having freedom wasn't just about money: it was also about having the time to enjoy it. But most of all, I realised that I didn't need any money. What? My mind was blown. I had no idea how this was even possible, so I signed up to some courses to discover more. After all, you only know what you know. And what I knew hadn't taken me far.

Investing in myself and getting some education was an absolute game-changer for me. Granted, I had to get into even more debt to find out how I could change my life, which was extremely scary at the time, but I was desperate. Thankfully, it worked, because within a couple of months of completing the course, I had managed to purchase my first property, despite not having any cash, and kept going until I was 'financially free'.

The truth is that you need 'big lady balls' to really change your life. I started with nothing, was massively in debt and felt that I was at rock bottom. But it was this burning desire to change my life that led to me taking massive action. Without it, would I have been desperate enough to jump in when the odds were well and truly against me?

I've met so many people who are in a much better position than I was when starting out, but still haven't managed to achieve much. This is largely because they let fear get in the way. They worry about whether it will work, or whether they will lose money. But here's the thing: I believe that you just need to 'feel the fear and do it anyway' and just get on with it. As long as you have the knowledge and have carried out your due diligence, what have you got to lose? Was I scared that it wouldn't work? Yes. Was I scared I would lose money that I didn't have? Of course. Did I do it anyway? Hell, yes. Doubt is perfectly natural, but you don't get anything in this life if you play it safe.

You can let your self-doubt get the better of you and stop you progressing in life, or you can charge on regardless and smash it. Personal development and filling your mind with things that help you to grow are essential. This is one of my favourite quotes:

"Whether you think you can, or you think you can't, you're right."

Henry Ford

This is so true. I had no idea how the hell I was going to turn my life around, but I believed that I could, so I did.

My aim is to empower women to take charge of their lives too, without getting massively in debt. If I can do it, anyone can. Let go of what isn't serving you and be brave enough to follow your dreams, the kind of dreams that you used to have when you were little, not the ones that have been squashed to comply with the norm.

The truth is that you'll need to make some sacrifices along the way, but as long as you're prepared to become uncomfortable to feel comfortable and to do whatever it takes, then it will happen.

The life of your dreams is waiting – you've just got to have courage to go out and get it.

If I can do it, so can you.

Lynsey Anne Toft

Lynsey Toft is an entrepreneur, property investor, coach and mentor. Her background is in teaching, but after having children she was desperate for more in her life. She now combines teaching and being an entrepreneur, with coaching others on how to improve their mindset and financial situation, to regain control of their lives and become financially free as part of the strategy she teaches through her company, Tidy Ventures.com.

Lynsey works with people from all walks of life, who all have one common goal: they all want more in life and want to have fun in the process. Whether the goal is to have another stream of income, replace an existing job or to create a retirement plan, Lynsey can help.

Lynsey is a wife and mother to two beautiful girls and four dogs and likes to live life to the fullest, as tomorrow is promised to no one. She works hard and plays hard and loves travelling and making memories with her family. Lynsey enjoys giving back and strives to help make the world a better place for our children.

www.tidyventures.com

INSPIRATIONAL WOMEN OF THE WORLD

13.
LOVE TO LEAD

Melissa Curran

I believe many leaders still have a long way to go when it comes to people leadership. The truth is that there are many people in organisations who lose the love for what they do because of the environment that a leader creates. The leader can make it the best place to go to work or one of the worst. Many people ask me how they can help their managers become better leaders. The solution, of course, is hard work and comes down to relationships. We are talking about leading from the heart. Quality relationships take work and it isn't just about spending time with the people we gravitate to the most.

I grew up in South Wales. When I was nine and my brother was seven, our mother started to 'ground' us for bad behaviour, sending us to our rooms. This typically resulted in my brother going to his room and pulling a rock star stunt – pulling the curtains down, putting his finger in a plug socket, pushing a piece of Lego up his nose, those sorts of things. While I, on the other hand, wasn't overly happy about being grounded either, I took it as an opportunity to turn on the cassette player and sing with the hairbrush in the mirror, thoroughly enjoying my time out. Well, until my mother soon caught on to this and took the cassette player away. Ha! It was good while it lasted.

This is one key memory of how I started to develop the skill of looking at something in a different way and adapting to change, staying positive. This ability can help us in our business and personal relationships.

Ask yourself this question: Do you love to lead? What about the people who are challenging in your teams? You know the ones: they don't do what others do, object to everything you encourage them to do, have a problem for every solution, turn up late to meetings, get defensive in feedback sessions or act dismissively. These people have the potential, they just do not seem to care enough, even though they may even be hitting the company targets that have been set.

There was, for the sake of this story, a gentleman called Valentine. Let me take you back 10 years. He had been on my team while working at a top, award-winning call centre in the UK. It had around 300 employees and we had both been there for about two years. Many people believe call centres are the factories of our time. Well, we were the best team in the company. Miles above the rest. Consistent and absolutely smashing targets. Everyone, or so I thought, should be happy. Valentine was always the more challenging team member, behaving differently. One day he asked to speak to me and the centre manager. He seemed nervous and then he came out with it, "I want to request to move team." Pause. Here is where my ego as a manager and leader took a big dent. Move team? Hello? We were the best team in the company!

There were two possible reactions to this (especially for the girl who liked to sing with her hairbrush):

1. The emotional response – supported by the Gloria Gaynor song, *I Will Survive*, "Go on now go, walk out the door, don't turn around now, you're not welcome anymore." Emotional,

I know. Send him packing, take it personally and be rid of his challenging ways.

2. The objective response – supported by the Queen song, *I Want to Break Free*. Free myself from the situation and my emotions to start to look at this objectively.

The thing is, no matter who we are, there will always be an emotional response first due to mirror neurons in our brains that mimic the response to one another, as part of our survival. A bit like when I take my dog for a walk: if we pass another dog with an aggressive stance, he will take an aggressive stance too. Let us pause at this emotional crossroads for a moment.

You see, your ability to love to lead is down to the art of connection. To get the secondary objective response and break free from the emotional response, here are three points to consider.

1. Observation versus evaluation – try to rise above how you feel about a person, above your likes or dislikes of that person.

2. Put yourself in their shoes – most people judge from their own point of view. Aiming to be less sensitive and more reflective will allow you to look at the situation from a different angle.

3. Overcome any tendency to grumble or criticise – stay positive and pause.

When we master these three points, liberating ourselves of the emotional response, it leads effectively to personal accountability.

So, back to the story, there he was asking to move team and I stood there, realising in that moment that it was the classic cliché from every relationship, "It's *me*, not *you*." It was my fault. I asked Valentine to think about his decision. I would reflect on it too, look at the options, then talk again in the morning. Here was my time to embrace humility, acknowledge my flaws and accept that I had a hand to play in this. When leaders acknowledge that they have flaws, they encourage their team members not to be afraid of making mistakes. Imagine the courage it had taken for him to approach me and ask the question, let alone the number of days beforehand he had spent unhappy.

All of us, including Valentine, have four big needs. We need to be of value, to be in control, to belong and to be safe. I had failed to support my team in these four big needs. The top two for him were to feel valued and to belong. How could I make him feel that he was in a team where he could belong when, as I realised, I knew hardly anything about him? I did not want to be a leader who made people feel like this.

The next day, I apologised. Showing vulnerability, I pointed out my flaws as a leader and said I was willing to fix or build our relationship for him to stay on the team, even though I recognised that he didn't feel he was a valued member of the team. Now I cared. Here was my journey from objection to affection, no longer all about the number, the taskmaster or just focused on the easiest people to work with. I had a passion for people. I paid more attention to Valentine, and even went to an open mic night that he organised, in my personal time. I found out that he wrote amazing poetic rap. Imagine his face when he saw that I had made the effort to be there. Thankfully, he stayed on the team.

Research tells us that when 4,000 people were surveyed 35% of them said they didn't have strong relationships at work. These are the ones who are looking for other jobs or, as in this story, considering moving teams before making a final decision to jump ship. That is a lot of people. These are people who when they joined the organisation were enthusiastic, happy and positive. Something happened along the way for that person to change. Maybe it was a life event; more often it is because the culture they bought into didn't exist, or when they had an idea they weren't listened to, or because they didn't have a great relationship with their manager.

Only 54% of employers believe that strong work relationships improve company culture. I want to tell you that this also improves our lives, our mentality and our overall wellbeing. What confuses me is the 46% of employers who don't believe it is important. We must change this. Think about the clients, teams you work with or your own team. Write or make a mental list of those people you work with daily. Go ahead.

Your Valentine is the person you just listed last or, even worse, forgot to think about at all. Let's be better! Do it for them, make them your focus, get to know them and take responsibility for your relationship. Ask more questions. Speak to them because you want to not just because you need something. Find out what they are passionate about and what truly motivates them.

You may be wondering, "Is Valentine still there?" No, he isn't. While he realised that I could change and love to lead, there were others in the organisation who were not like that. You may work for a company or run a company where leaders *do* love to lead. The ability to love to lead is not a nice to have, it's a must have!

Thanks for reading and thanks to Valentine for a lesson I will never forget.

Melissa Curran

Melissa Curran has a passion for people, which has been her driving motivation for the last 20 years. She founded the Modern Mind Group and is driven by emotion to empower others with a mission of "emotioneering to change the hearts and minds of at least one million people for the better".

Melissa has worked for over five years as a trusted, global business management consultant, working with high-profile organisations in leadership, operational excellence and culture transformation. Having battled with anxiety, depression, burnout and grief, Melissa uses these valuable insights in her roles as an advocate for mental health and a trained counsellor to motivate and inspire change.

As a motivational speaker, Melissa is captivating, because of her special capacity for empathy, which engages the audience from the heart.

She lives in Wales with her husband, Stephen, and their French bulldog, and her leisure pursuits include playing volleyball and paddle boarding.

INSPIRATIONAL WOMEN OF THE WORLD

14.

TESTAMENT TO RESILIENCE

Rachel Brydon

The image conjured up when you hear the words 'alcohol-dependent' is not the reality for most people who are. And rarely included are the family and friends who are massively affected by the addiction and should also be in the picture. The societal impacts of addictions on the lives of children are well documented, and I want to share how I created a personal mission to negate the impact of substance misuse, not only on my own child, but on the lives of many children.

The father of my child is alcohol-dependent. There, I've said it. I rarely say it out loud as it has its own stigma. Over the last five years I have made peace with the fact that it is not my guilt to carry. I've learned to be proud of the integrity and values I hold, which helped me to survive living with an addict and ultimately to thrive.

I am not an 'in the home drinker'. I've just never been bothered by a glass of wine to unwind or something fizzy to celebrate. I do drink, but socially, which means I go months between drinks. However, my ex-partner was a massive drinker but I thought he predominantly drank with friends and when he visited his home town for overnight stays. Looking back, I can now identify so many warning signs, but you don't know until you know. The point of my 'knowing' came around the time I was giving birth, five years ago. When you are on maternity leave and spending significantly more time at home, it gets harder to avoid seeing the signs.

Being the responsible partner and mother that I am, I encouraged my partner to seek help as soon as I recognised what was happening. When my baby was just eight months old, I had pleaded with the community substance misuse team so much; it had not been seen as a priority because he was still managing to work, but they agreed to bring our case to the top of the queue and do an assessment. A medical detox was prescribed. A medical detox is recommended only when the risk of immediately stopping the alcohol use can cause withdrawal symptoms as severe as death. Simply put, to be prescribed this, you must be reliant on alcohol to function. I was elated. We were getting the help needed more quickly, and after the detox process he would have access to a strong prescription drug that made the body react to any alcohol – a helpful deterrent. Or so I thought.

Just one month before I returned to work from maternity leave, the signs were there again. I found letters about missed Community Alcohol and Drug Team appointments and stashed supplies of the prescribed drugs, which were meant to be taken daily. The weekend before I was due back at work, the baby and I had been locked out of our home by my partner, as he had passed out drunk, having forgotten to take his keys out of the door on the inside. It was 2pm.

There were many instances of this happening over the following year. Other things that you'd expect too, like finding bottles stashed, dinners ruined thanks to the oven being left on for hours while he was unconscious, and many, many incidents of him urinating on the bed and sofa while in an inebriated state. What I hadn't prepared for though were the lies. Living with an addict, I learned that lying becomes so instinctive that lies about everyday life are endemic.

No amount of pleading or reasoning was having an impact, so we lived entirely separate lives. To the outside world, we looked almost normal. Except that new mum friends I made were never invited back to the house for fear of what I would be presented with. When other mums started going out for the day with friends and leaving the dads to bond with their babies, I could never participate, nor could I explain why. Many conversations no doubt took place in my absence about how I did not allow myself the opportunity to have some much-needed downtime and fun by telling the dad to step up, or to give him a chance. It was only natural, after all; they didn't know my reluctance was based on his capacity rather than typical new mum control issues.

That was the paradoxical position in which I quite often found myself. Having to shoulder blame for 'my' choices by not feeling able to share a deeply personal and upsetting reality. Blame is an interesting concept, and the guilt felt by me, and I'm sure others in my situation, is multi-faceted.

There were two or three friends who knew. They were friends who didn't have children and couldn't see past the black and white nature of stay or go. While well-meaning in intention, every single one of those conversations in which I had to defend still living in the same home hurt me more than I ever shared. I felt totally without allies. On one hand, I had new mum friends who didn't know and couldn't understand why I was doing everything solo; and on the other, friends of old who couldn't tolerate the situation on my behalf and told me exactly what they wanted me to do, with no consideration of the impact it was having on me during those conversations, or for when I was to become a one-income household. Both groups really were just trying to get me to be happy, and although I understood that, it didn't stop me feeling alone.

Some of the hardest conversations for me to navigate were with members of his family who didn't recognise the extent of the problem, despite being aware of the medical detox and issues that I had to deal with as a consequence of the drinking at home. "Why don't you just talk to him?" or "I don't know why he does it." I have a great sense of fairness so felt compelled to explain that he was not in control: the alcohol was. That it wasn't personal, and I didn't hold him responsible for his addiction. My resilience, with my calm and logical manner, was partly the issue though. I didn't cause any arguments, nor did I wail about the unfairness of the situation. I just quietly got on with the business of keeping myself and my baby safe by leading an entirely separate life. My child is five now, and he has never been cared for by his father or spent time alone with him.

The turning point for me came one week when the cumulative impact of toddlerhood (meaning I couldn't easily keep us in one room), an increase in aggression and goading while he was inebriated, and an absolute verbal assault on my parenting choices became too much. I believe in attachment parenting and being responsive to your child, and my professional life and personal identity were bound in those values. It was the first time I had ever responded and been drawn into an argument with him while he was drunk, and in that exchange I made the decision to tell him to leave. I realised how scared I had been, living at home with an addict, and that the balance had tipped in terms of what I could endure to be financially stable. My resilience had been tested and stretched and I had to make a change before it was depleted. I asked him to move out. The relief was palpable for me.

In my career, I was keenly aware of the impact a parent with an addiction could have on a child. I saw it as my sole responsibility to mitigate every adverse childhood experience (ACE) point the situation gave my child; and to provide an environment that allowed him to flourish. Knowing that one point of trauma does not have to define a lifetime is powerful. I also knew the science behind all my parenting choices: how I interact, explain and involve him. I kept family life a haven for him, which has allowed him to bloom into a confident, well adjusted, resilient and tenacious child.

Through all this, I was also quietly building a business, as well as working and managing keeping us safe. I was providing training to organisations and community classes for children, geared towards increasing resilience, enabling empowerment of choices and promoting wellbeing.

This personal experience galvanised my resolve to support children in every way I could. I had initially focused on working with children, yet through a series of opportunities and professional connections, it quickly became apparent that my path was to train professionals. Having written and facilitated many training courses throughout my career, it was a natural step.

I know that by promoting emotion coaching in the home and in interactions with children, I am having a direct, positive effect on the lives of thousands of children. In delivering wellbeing training to professionals, I am having an impact not just on their professional lives, but their home lives too. I love the ripple effect I am putting out into the world, and I am even more grateful for the choices I have been able to make that have shaped my favourite child in the universe to be the awesome, resilient child he is.

Rachel Brydon

Rachel Brydon is the founder of Calm in the Chaos Training, Consultancy and Community Services. In a career spanning 20 years in social services, youth services and the third sector, Rachel has worked with the most vulnerable children and families. This has cemented her passion to create waves and ripples that have a positive impact for children, and on family life; it underpins the training and mentoring programmes she has created and facilitated.

Rachel enjoys taking complex neuroscience and findings about mental wellbeing, and breaking them down into practical strategies for children and adults to use. She believes that it has to make sense to them in their own lives, so that it will be applied.

Rachel is best described as a pragmatic optimist and a naturally positive person. You are as likely to find her delivering training in a conference suite as you are to find her on a deadlift platform. She is commonly found drinking massive mugs of tea while pretending to do admin.

www.calminthechaos.co.uk

www.linkedin.com/in/rachelbrydon

15.
RAGS TO RICHES

Sandra Blake

I'd always been told that I didn't 'need' a university education. My father told me all I had to do was find a husband, have children and that I would be fulfilled. Really? Looking back now, it's hard to think about how this expectation was so embedded in women of my generation.

I left school at 17 and started my first job. By 22, I was married. Goal reached. By the time I was 27, I had five children and very limited experience of work.

I was happy with my life, but we struggled. We lived in a comfortable four-bedroom council house and making ends meet was tough. The constant pressure to meet the needs and expectations of my growing children was relentless. Time disappeared. I wanted more, and I wanted it to be *easier*. With my husband on permanent nights as a taxi driver, the role of looking after the children was mine. Was my father right after all?

I began investigating. The more I read about what other people were doing and their success, I wondered whether I could do it. I wanted a better life for us – to be able to give my children every opportunity in life. To have time – time to enjoy my family, my husband. But I procrastinated. I doubted myself. I wasted time. Looking back, I should have pushed harder.

Six years later – I won't go into what happened in those six years, but without these wrong turns I wouldn't be the woman I am today – I started a weekend job in a call centre for a buy and sell weekly magazine. Think Facebook marketplace in print.

Now this next bit is important.

While I was working there, my father gave me a portable gas fire. No idea why, but he obviously thought it would come in handy. It wasn't for me, so I advertised it. With seven responses in 24 hours after the weekly release, I quickly realised that if I bought more, I could sell more, and for some reason unbeknown to me, gas fires were in demand. The next week I placed an advertisement asking for portable gas fires. I received 12 calls and purchased 12 gas fires. At the same time, I had also advertised a portable gas fire for sale. My buyers were already lined up. I did this for several weeks and realised that if it worked for gas fires, it would work for other things.

The achievement. The excitement. The buzz.

The selling continued and I was successful. With faith in myself, I took the next step, the next risk. I opened a shop selling second-hand baby equipment and clothes. Every week I scoured the boot sales, second-hand stores and charity shops and bought everything that I thought would sell. I'd take them home, wash them, iron them and put them for sale in my shop. The business grew quickly, but I was struggling with time management and looking after the children. I needed to find a balance. Somebody mentioned to me I could get an au pair.

Welcome to Angelise. She lived in and was an absolute godsend.

From Monday to Friday, while I was at work, Angelise looked after the children. She cleaned and she cooked. It was starting to feel easier. When I arrived home from work, I had quality time with the children before they went to bed. I had missed this.

Here is what I consider to be my next milestone. My daughter was about to start high school and the schools in our area weren't where I wanted any of our children to go. My husband and I decided we would send her to private school. It would stretch us hugely, but we felt this was not something we were willing to compromise on. We knew if we did this for her, we would have to do it for all our children. We were fully committed to doing this and make the necessary sacrifices. This was one of the best decisions we ever made. Life was better, and we had also reached another milestone – owning our own home.

Completely by chance, I was given a leaflet about university degree courses. A change in direction. I thought a degree would give me success. I applied, but my application was rejected because I didn't have the qualifications for entry. Another option was to take a foundation course, which would give me the qualifications I needed to get accepted on to the degree course. More work. More time. More delays. After two years of hard studying, I passed and finally was able to start my degree. I went on to study housing and graduated in 1999. I was thrilled. But where next?

I attended lots of interviews, and was rejected every time, either because I had no work experience or because my degree meant I was over-qualified. Eventually I was offered a job with the council. I loved this job, absolutely loved it. I thrived and in four years had climbed the ladder there before landing an even better role with a housing association. It still wasn't enough.

By this time, we'd moved again, into our 'forever home' and it was like a dream come true. But in the process, we had taken on a huge mortgage. With the success had come more responsibility. In 2003, I went home and told my husband that I'd handed in my notice and I was going to open my own letting agency. He wasn't pleased. And to be honest, I think we almost got a divorce. This was make or break. Within three months, I had my own agency and we started to buy property and build our own lettings portfolio.

In 2008, the property recession hit and hit us hard. We struggled but came through it. Now came my partner in crime. My eldest son left school. He was 17 and decided that he wanted to join me in the family business. My husband also decided he wanted to spend more time with the family and came onboard. Everything was coming together.

Having my own agency, I have had the opportunity to work with many people. I'm a big believer in self-development. I started teaching landlords how to be better landlords, albeit for free. I started giving advice on how to build a property portfolio just as I had done, and along the way, I helped a lot of people build successful businesses. I love inspiring and empowering people to become cash-comfortable and lead better lives. I feel achievement. I feel my own success through theirs, yours.

Fast forward to 2016 and the property market had changed dramatically. The world had changed. Online had already exploded and Facebook and Instagram offered new marketing platforms. You needed to become informed or be left behind. I found a mentor and undertook training. From this, I've grown a successful coaching and mentoring business, Sandra Blake Coaching, where I inspire and help others to build their own success. I've gone from scraping by to having a multimillion-pound property portfolio and a successful letting agency. I've taken my family from living in a council house to living in a beautiful home worth over £1m. But most importantly of all, I've inspired all my children to believe in their own success.

This year, 2020, has brought challenges for everybody, but it's also opened doors. If you're feeling that you want more, go for it. Don't wait and especially don't wait for the 'right time'. Ask yourself what you truly want to do with the rest of your life. Time doesn't wait for anyone and before you know it another year has passed, and you are wondering, "What if?"

Think of it like this – are your biggest regrets the things you did do? Or those things you didn't?

I know you probably have a million doubts – going through your responsibilities, thinking about the risks, what will people think, what happens if it doesn't work, was it all for nothing? Believe me when I say that was me. But I couldn't continue thinking every day, "Is this it?"

I have been there. I am not telling you it's plain sailing. You need to work at it, know your own mind and understand what you want, but I am here to help you. There will be haters, and social media can be cruel, but don't let the fear hold you back. It may seem scary, but it isn't half as scary as when you just do it.

My advice is always to learn from the best: attend the best courses and the best seminars that you can afford. Listen intently. Ask sincere questions.

One of my mentors said, "If you want to be rich and successful, surround yourself with rich, successful people." Believe that dreams can come true, because if they could come true for me, they certainly can for you.

> ## "If you don't risk anything, you risk everything."
>
> **Rob Moore**

Sandra Blake

Sandra Blake is a highly respected estate agent and co-owner of a multiple award-winning estate and letting agency, and has a multi-million-pound property portfolio.

She owns The Unstoppable Agent, a leading online business coaching programme that leverages scalable strategies for estate and letting agents to successfully grow their businesses to become cash-comfortable.

With over 30 years' experience in the property industry and a degree in housing, Sandra has developed a myriad of skills and wealth of experience.

Through Sandra Blake Coaching, she uses her fundamental knowledge and comprehensive understanding of property and business, inspiring and motivating others to build, grow and develop their own businesses.

Sandra's career as an entrepreneur has included starting, buying, financing, selling and building six-figure businesses, providing her with multiple revenue streams.

https://harryharper.co.uk/

IWOW
INSPIRATIONAL WOMEN OF THE WORLD

16.
A MINDSET REVIVAL

Sheena Ytil

Traumatic events can encompass anything from sexual assault or childhood abuse to mental health crises. When trauma occurs in childhood it is likely to affect your adult life, because it happens at a time when the brain is vulnerable. Experiences of divorce, car accidents, emotional, physical, verbal and sexual abuse, childhood instability, domestic violence and neglect are events that trigger emotional and even physical reactions. They can also make you prone to other health conditions. People who experience trauma struggle with getting help because they want to avoid thinking about it. In many cases, defence mechanisms are created, such as denial or normalising the past.

My parents did their best to make life as comfortable as possible for their five kids. My mum was a stay-at-home mother and my dad worked in construction. In good times and bad I have always admired my mum and never really noticed that a lot of my caring, loving, nurturing and selflessness characteristics, even my sternness, come directly from her. We went through some tough times, especially when my dad was sent off to work on another island. Thank God for our tuck shop, which kept us going. There were also times of verbal and physical abuse, which were called 'disciplining'.

My mum often opened our home to people who needed help. I recall her housing a single mum, with a daughter and grandson. My mum nurtured them the same way she nurtured us. I was grateful for that family, because when puberty arrived, I was unprepared and panicked. Thankfully, I was able to speak with our house guest.

Although some forms of verbal and physical love and affection were absent from the home, there was still love and care – we were nurtured, fed, sheltered, educated and looked after at home. However, communication was lacking with my parents, and this was an issue I worked on when I got older.

For a short while, we experienced homelessness and stayed in a church (we grew up deeply religious). Because of my mum's pride, she would not accept or ask for help from family, but we sometimes visited food banks at the weekend. She worked hard to care for us, but struggled at times because she was ill. During her times of ailment, I raised my siblings. I was a child myself, but I could not turn a blind eye, and took on the responsibility. At the time I was unaware of how this experience affected me, negatively and positively,

I started working in my junior year of high school, around the same time my grandma moved in with us. I continued working into my senior year and never stopped. I proved myself to be resourceful and dependable in all I did. The pressure of responsibilities at home, a job and focusing on school was intense. I was quick to finish my assignments so that I could mentally plan my after-school objectives. They stemmed from prepping dinner, washing uniforms, assisting mum and grandma with meds and doctor visits, in addition to any homework that my siblings and I had. Sometimes it was taxing because there was no electricity or running water. Ladies from the church would come and assist with those objectives, which helped.

In my primary school years and onwards, an after-school programme called The Indaba Project and my grandmother were a major help. My grandmother and I were close, so when she died, I was despondent. The Indaba Project was a haven from my overwhelming life. The director himself became a major part of my support system, at that time and beyond. I also became a volunteer for that programme, to give back.

My grades seesawed so much in junior school that my teachers noticed and inquired into my family life. In secondary school, I refocused and improved my grades. I was punctual and proudly carried out my duties as a prefect. On my walks to school, I sometimes placed my lunch money in the hands of homeless people. I was always open to helping others, even when I was withdrawn and quiet.

I was often in survival mode mentally and did not realise it. I tried to always ensure that my siblings and I could attend school, but sometimes we could not because of the things we lacked. I had only one friend and I had little desire to go out, plus I was not allowed to. I was shy and in my head most of the time – the observant and over-analytical young girl who kept everyone at a distance, even though my reputation was that of a popular nerd.

I tried to commit suicide twice, overdosing on drugs and poison. I survived but hallucinated for weeks. Thoughts of sexual molestation by a family member, previously suppressed, resurfaced gradually, which made my mental state worse. The pressure was immense and came from all angles: home, my studies, national exams and fulfilling other requirements to graduate. I had an emotional breakdown during my final exams. I was removed and unable to finish.

When I was 19, I started house-sitting in the western suburbs. I used that opportunity to get out of the house for peace of mind, privacy, tranquillity and self-development. I had chronic insomnia. My weight vacillated and my pillows were drenched from tears most nights. In my early 20s, all my courses, including my continued pharmaceutical studies, were also a challenge, but I pushed through. I was in bad debt and my work environment was toxic. My manager at my third job was very intimidated by me, which resulted in ill-treatment from him.

I have come to better understand how powerful the subconscious mind is and how it frames how we live, even when our conscious selves are striving to make changes. I have started to perceive things differently and put them into practice by creating habits to refurbish my memory chip.

Over the past few years, every time I accomplished something or was working on a goal, it came to a standstill and fell flat. I have learned to pick myself up every time because I am determined to create a change for myself. That meant fighting myself sometimes daily from self-sabotage. I believe that we all can change our present-day experience of our past experiences by discovering ways to revitalise our mindset.

Tools I used to heal and reprogramme my mind:

1. I started with self-motivation because I was fighting what seemed like a losing battle with myself mentally.

2. I found peace in helping others and using the beach as a form of therapy.

3. I got professional help to heal the pain of my past trauma and create new self-care habits.

4. I exercised and watched my diet.

5. I created life charts and vision boards, and practised meditation.

6. I focused on my breathing, writing letters and audio love notes to myself.

7. I started reading, listening to my favourite motivational speakers and to TED Talks, practising self-care and going outside my comfort zone.

8. I let go of toxic friendships.

9. I released expectations and chose to be happy amid my adversity.

10. I practised using empowering affirmations:

    o I *am* confident, healthy, and fearless. I am not my past.

    o I *have* great support, abundant joy, peace and willingness.

    o I *feel* appreciated, empowered, content, relaxed.

Transformation I experienced after revitalising my mindset

1. Seeing my vision boards gave me motivation; they allowed me to exercise my imagination and kept me focused on my plans and goals. They cheered me up when I felt melancholy and dejected, and helped me work through periods of procrastination. My mindset stayed positive and my doubts and self-sabotaging thoughts were minimised.

2. Working on my healing helped me to clarify what I wanted for my life, and forced me to put my thoughts and dreams on paper, therefore making them more real in my mind. It helped me to see them as possible.

3. Practising affirmations helped free me from negative self-talk, such as settling for the mediocre. It boosted my self-confidence and helped me identify the limitations that I placed on myself.

4. Self-reflection helps me clarify my values, deepen my understanding of self, and develop higher-level thinking that could better identify the root causes of my complex issues.

5. Writing letters helped me to fathom the power and strength within me. I wrote gratitude letters, and journaled about what I deserved, what I was proud of, what I forgave myself for, and what I was committed to.

Ultimately, I have been able to stop doubting myself; quit putting things off; quit thinking I have no choice; quit doing the same things repeatedly and expecting a different result; quit feeding my past energy; quit thinking everything will work out on its own; quit saying, "Yes," when I mean "No."

Despite the many downward spirals from my mental trauma, my healing journey has led to a mindset revival.

Sheena Ytil

Sheena Ytil works in the tourism industry, where she coordinates the identification of hazards, inspects and evaluates the workplace, and implements procedures for compliance with corporate and government health and safety standards and regulations for large resorts.

She is a speaker and mentor to young girls, boys and women who have been through challenges in their childhood, helping them rehabilitate their mindset from traumatising experiences and conditioning.

Sheena is a mindfulness app ambassador, certified life coach (The Mindset Revival), virtual assistant to a nutritionist, and a freelance market researcher. She owns a personal assistant concierge business, Second Set of Hands, and a retail business. She also founded a not-for-profit organisation providing meals and groceries to elderly people in need.

Sheena is a humanitarian and environmentalist who is passionate about raising awareness and creating a forum for mental health healing. She volunteers with numerous non-governmental organisations (NGOs) and in her free time enjoys boating, writing, visiting beaches, travelling and girl talk.

IWOW
INSPIRATIONAL WOMEN OF THE WORLD

17.
WEIGHT NO MORE

Suzanne Burnell-Watts

My unique approach, intuitive thinking and ability to dip into my skill box play an important part in helping me create a safe environment for myself and my clients to work in. A great number of them come through personal recommendations.

Such was the case of Chloe, who I was asked to contact after her many years of struggling with depression, anxiety, loss and much more. It was now time to unburden herself of 'the secret' which was consuming her more each day, to the point where she now felt she was drowning and needed rescuing.

The first contact with Chloe, instigated at her request, lasted just 30 minutes. It threw up weight issues, which I recognised were driven by a deeper psychology. The gamechanger in this call was when I assured her that she did not have to trawl over her back story for me to help her. Each client needs a different approach in tackling the paradox of dealing with Pandora's box and in this case, I felt I should trust my intuition and tread very gently.

Something had happened in Chloe's life between the ages of 9 and 14 that taught her to behave in ways that had become normal to her. She had continued the same patterns of behaviour for her whole life – that is, until we started making changes. She had developed the ability to suppress her feelings, avoid confrontation and release her emotions only when alone, which often led to long periods of isolation.

I phoned Chloe once a week to see how we could reduce the chaos that was so predominant in her life. She first needed to learn to take care of herself again, after years of self-neglect. This still continues and I see her, a year on, as a beacon of hope to others going through similar situations. I quickly became aware that the flashbacks she was suffering from prevented her from sleeping upstairs in her bed. We needed to take baby steps so as not to make her feel overwhelmed. I made a personalised hypnosis for her to listen to at night, when she slept on her sofa. Chloe's feedback was that the recordings made the nights a little less lonely, and the content of them began to have positive effects.

As Chloe opened up in our phone conversations, she shared the fact she had lost her dad when she was 25. Although heartbroken, she never showed it as she put all of her strength into helping her mum come to terms with her own loss. Shortly after this she became a mother to a beautiful daughter, not once but twice. The birth of her girls brought her love and joy but she began to struggle with the weight of her grief and untold secret. Chloe's relationship with her partner began to break down, but this made her even more determined to pretend that everything was OK. Now, alone with her children, everything came to a head, for the first time in her life and she could not see a way forward.

Chloe tells me, "I was no longer able to pretend, and didn't have the energy to try anymore. I could be practical and look after the children and their needs, but everything else fell apart. It was as though I was paralysed, but not in my body. It was from within as if my soul were trapped. I lost all concept of consequences. I wasn't paying the bills or even aware of what was going out of my bank account. I would go all day without thinking about eating or drinking, until the evening, when I would suddenly feel unwell and eat large amounts of snack type food, rather than cook. I would cook for the girls earlier in the evening but never ate with them. I avoided being in their company for long, as I desperately did not want them to see I wasn't OK. If I didn't find comfort in food of an evening, I would drink alcohol until I fell asleep."

Hitting rock bottom, Chloe saw a doctor but still refused to share any secrets, and was prescribed medication for anxiety and depression. This took the edge off but didn't solve her problem. She got a referral to see a counsellor, this was not a positive experience, because she knew within minutes of her meeting that she was not going to be honest with this person about her past, so it felt pointless.

During the year we have chatted, we have unravelled historic abuse, secrets, low self-esteem, post-traumatic stress disorder (PTSD), anxiety, eating problems, relationship and bonding worries, grief, loneliness and feelings of isolation. No wonder Chloe was unable to function or work full-time. Unfortunately, anxiety is not always the result of just one negative event, it is often the result of a combination of many and the body can no longer store them.

I encouraged Chloe to email me any time with her thoughts and feelings and there were many. As her confidence grew, so did the clarity of the content. I listened carefully, not just to what was emailed or spoken, but also to the silent omissions, the process was gentle, and Chloe set the pace for recovery. I needed her to have some structure in her life, and we set about doing this in a way that was manageable for her and her children. The flashbacks were becoming more and more vivid as she started opening up, so I used her words to tap into her subconscious mind and allow her to dissociate from the dreams. With each problem we unwrapped I recorded a personalised hypnosis for her to listen to each night, her feedback was, "Your voice alone was like an audio-hug, if there is such a thing."

A breakthrough came for me when I spoke about the girls and their ages. Her voice immediately reverted to that of a child. I knew I had hit on 'the Secret', without realising quite what it was. This was my opportunity to open the door to her sharing her childhood with me. Chloe couldn't speak openly and preferred to write long emails, almost as if writing were not the same as speaking out. Discovering that the historic abuse had occurred at the same age her girls were now was the catalyst which allowed me to be more specific about the way I would deal with moving forward. We needed to acknowledge, accept, thank and let go of the trauma. I used hypnotherapy and Time Line Therapy (TLT), alongside some cognitive behavioural therapy (CBT) and a large helping of neurolinguistic programming (NLP).

As the weeks passed, Chloe's voice became stronger and her mindset appeared brighter. We reached a stage when she felt able to apply for a full-time job, which would have been unimaginable just eight months before. We talked through the process and I recorded a hypnosis for self-confidence and owning her space in the interview. Chloe got the job.

The lockdown in 2020 could not have happened at a better time for Chloe. While she isolated with the girls at home, we talked through healthy eating, planning meals and menus, organising her time and clearing space. She set a routine and organised plenty of activities with the girls. Their dogs needed to be walked and this became their daily exercise as a family. She had time to work on herself with no interruptions.

The bedroom, in which she now feels comfortable and relaxed has had a makeover and each morning she wakes up feeling rested. Chloe tells me that her new job is good and has prospects. She is working through her finances and tackling any debts. Her home is now a happy home where she is present and engaged with her girls. Her personality is returning, which I know is a big thing for her, as she did not like the person she had become and missed herself very much.

Chloe's own words were, "To have someone treat you as though you are so valuable, when you are feeling so worthless is amazing medicine in itself, but better than that, you didn't tell me I was wrong to feel worthless; you just taught me to see myself in a different way. You had this amazing confidence in your voice that didn't 'suggest' things were going to be OK, but 'told' me they were absolutely 100% going to be OK, and I needed to hear that, without realising it. What I have learned has been life-changing".

Now working in a great job Chloe is not just surviving but thriving. She visited her doctor, who has written a plan to slowly reduce her medications. Living in an organised, happy home with a clear mind and forming new positive habits has enabled her to lose a stone during lockdown.

She sees this as the beginning, a chance to be the mother she set out to be and to continue discovering the best version of herself, and finally, a future.

Suzanne Burnell-Watts

Suzanne Burnell-Watts is an expert within the field of clinical hypnotherapy. She is highly sought after and respected in the industry and her qualifications include Train the Trainer, Master Practitioner in neurolinguistic programming (NLP), Time Line Therapy (TLT), reiki and sound therapy.

Suzanne is also a registered HypnoBand (virtual gastric band) practitioner and has worked nationally and internationally with a wide range of clients. She regularly speaks about hypnotherapy on the radio and at various events throughout the UK.

Suzanne's passion and unique approach to her clients' needs over the past 20 years are reflected in her testimonials, which pay tribute to her knowledge, compassion and ability to change lives, while still recognising the difficulties and traumas her clients are going through. She is a true inspiration to all who cross her path.

www.lifechange4u.co.uk

http://www.linkedin.com/in/suzanneburnellwatts

INSPIRATIONAL WOMEN OF THE WORLD

18.
OVERCOMING ADVERSITY

Toni Clarkstone

Throughout life, one of the biggest hurdles we face is overcoming adversity and I have had my fair share from divorce and redundancy, all the way to physical and mental abuse, depression and cancer, as well as a long line of other health conditions starting from age 13. This chapter will give you a snapshot of a life-changing moment of adversity that took place in 2013 and will affect me for the rest of my life. I will explain the steps I took to overcome this and all the other adversities in my life and why I believe all the adverse experiences I've had over the years have made me successful in sales.

I grew up in a poor, single-parent household, where one year my mum was struggling so much that she contacted the Salvation Army and they came round with Christmas presents for us. I would watch my mum monitoring every penny she spent and walk around with holes in her shoes. So, growing up I was determined I would never struggle as she did. When I had my children, Luke and Joshua, I made it my mission never to let them go without and always to support them on life's journey.

But, as my mum had, I ended up a single parent. The difference was that I had worked my way up into a senior managerial role and was financially in a great position. I was working 50 hours a week and every day I felt guilty because I was missing out on my children's lives. I began to feel as though I was working myself into an early grave, with pain radiating throughout my body. The pain and the guilt persisted until I could take no more.

Then suddenly I was made redundant after eight years of working in the asset finance division of the bank. Although I was concerned about finances, I felt that a higher power knew I needed a break. I decided to become a sales consultant, coach and trainer, because I had gained coaching and leadership qualifications as well as becoming a qualified trainer when I was working in asset finance.

A new chapter was beginning in my life and it was great. I could finally spend quality time with my children, while still feeling that sense of achievement in my work. I began working with clients on creating more revenue through relationship selling, and it was proving successful, but what I could not understand was why I was still feeling the pain.

I was working great hours with great people and helping my clients achieve their goals, which gave me purpose, but still I was suffering. Things began to get worse and each day I was in excruciating pain. It finally resulted in me needing help from my family. I struggled to wash my hair and do the simplest of things. Each time I went to the doctor, they would just prescribe strong pain killers and never wanted to investigate the cause. Until one day it all became too much, and I let them have it. Finally, I was taken seriously and sent to the Queen Elizabeth Hospital Birmingham, where I met Dr Filer. He was amazing; he really took the time to listen and then arranged all the scans and tests for that day. After a five-hour appointment, I got my answer, but it was not the answer I was expecting. They told me I had rheumatoid arthritis, hypermobility syndrome and fibromyalgia.

After receiving the diagnosis, I sat down with the nurse to start lifetime medication and discuss the long-term effects of this debilitating condition. They had said, "Rheumatoid arthritis is serious – it's progressive and relentless." It suddenly became one of the hardest moments of my life. All my suffering over the last four years was suddenly explained. Yes, it was hard to hear, but I felt a sense of relief at finally having a diagnosis. They started me on a series of disease-modifying drugs, and I had to learn how to give myself injections.

The previous four years had been an emotional roller coaster and, in that moment, I had a choice to make. I could take stock of the situation and deal with the pain or sit around feeling sorry for myself. I had done enough of feeling sorry for myself in the past, so I was not going to let this stop me.

Once I started the medication, things started to clear up, but the side effects made me unwell. Weight gain, hair loss and fatigue – but the worst part was the nausea. After six months or so life started to get better; I had lost three stone, walked every day and had gone back to work.

Yes, I still had my bad days, but when I struggled to walk or cut my own food, I would focus on my goals and visualise achieving them.

Six months after my diagnosis, one of my goals became reality. It was totally unexpected, because part of me still thought my illness would put a man off, but it happened, like magic. I found my soulmate, Andrew, an ex-military man, who is amazing. I instantly fell for him and was so surprised at how well he adjusted to my world. We got married two years later and have been together for seven wonderful years.

Love was a powerful healer and daily life became easier. I will not pretend that my pains just disappeared, because they didn't, but I developed strategies to make life easier.

You see, I genuinely believe all the hardship I have experienced throughout my life has helped me be successful in the field of sales. One of the main ingredients of success in sales is resilience. When faced with a difficult situation, a salesperson must stand their ground. It's ultimately their determination and ability to handle rejection that will determine their success.

Over the years, the adversities have become a great teacher and I have gained a valuable insight into who I am. Some of the strategies I teach in sales can help everyone, but it's important to remember that change doesn't happen overnight.

The first step is to take stock of the situation and all you have been through with a clear mind. Reflection is an excellent way of building confidence and strength, as you are demonstrating to yourself that you have the capability to handle whatever is thrown at you.

The next step is to let go of what you cannot control; a good salesperson knows how to accept loss and focus on the next win. They simply let go of what was and have the confidence to believe in what will be. But the key is to adopt a growth mindset, which means that you must believe that you can develop and improve. Without this, you will continue to live in fear of the next challenge that life throws at you.

Once you have taken stock, reflected, and let go of what you cannot control with a growth mindset, you can start taking action in five easy steps.

Set your goals and make sure they are meaningful. I cannot stress how important this is. If it were not for my goals, I would have curled up and wasted most of my life, living in fear. By having a passion for your goals, you will motivate yourself to push forward and be successful.

Visualisation is also especially important. I get my clients to take time every day to visualise success and feel the excitement and joy that they will experience when achieving their goals. It has been scientifically proven that the brain cannot tell the difference between an image and reality. I use this tool to win big clients, as well as handling the adversities that have rocked me.

Surround yourself with like-minded people. A great place to start is networking and joining groups like IWOW. I believe that when you invest in personal or professional relationships, it can pay dividends throughout the course of your life.

Get a mentor who will keep you focused on your goals. They are an important part of personal and professional development and are excellent at providing support and guidance. It is important, however, to ensure that the mentor you choose is an expert in their field and has the experience to support you.

Be consistent and believe in yourself. As you go through this process, you will naturally start believing in yourself, and like a muscle, your ability to handle difficult situations and rejection will become stronger over time. Being consistent holds this all together and is the difference between success and failure. Great salespeople know that consistency creates accountability, reputation and relevance, which, in my opinion, is what all people want to feel, regardless of whether they work in sales or not.

It's important to remember that adversities may hurt for a while, but they will make you stronger and smarter, so embrace them.

Toni Clarkstone

Toni Clarkstone is an author, speaker and trainer who writes and lectures on relationship sales, customer loyalty and personal development. She works for one of the world's largest freight forwarders and has just been recognised as the top sales professional in Europe. She is a highly respected sales coach, mentor and trainer, and has been mentored by Grant Cardone.

She is passionate about helping and developing people with spheres of influence and achieving their true potential by selling value first and looking after their clients. Toni works with growth-oriented business owners and corporate companies that seek tailored executive coaching, mentoring and tailored training programmes for their employees.

Toni is a member of the International Authority for Professional Coaching and Mentoring (IAPC&M). It is her mission to educate and motivate sales teams and entrepreneurs for their growth and success.

19.
TO BE CONTINUED

Tracy Hill

> "It's 2002, my life as I knew it
> changed forever."

Life has a funny way of throwing you a curve ball now and then. And my life has certainly done this on more than one occasion. But this time, it was horrendous. It was life-changing beyond belief.

To the outside world, our life was perfect – we were living the dream. We had the detached house, a company car, good jobs, two children and another on the way – life was good. This was going to be our lovely family, complete.

Then I went into labour with my third child.

My little boy Oliver came into the world. His skin was perfect, and his thick dark hair beautiful. But our little boy was born with a rare condition, which meant us uprooting and going to Great Ormond Street Hospital for the foreseeable future. He was born at Cardiff University Hospital of Wales (UHW), and his little life was being threatened. I was scared. I was the most scared I had ever been in my entire life. Fear is an emotion that twists your thoughts and your whole view of the world as you know it.

The doctors called us into the family room to give us some news. This had become a regular occurrence. We were still at the Neonatal Intensive Care Unit (NICU) at Cardiff UHW at this point.

"We are afraid that we can no longer give your son the care he needs," they said. "We have contacted the staff at Great Ormond Street Hospital, and they have a special team of intensive care doctors coming to transfer him to London."

"How do you feel about this?" they asked. "We think it will be his only hope. You see he needs specialist treatment. We think he will be put on to a machine (ECMO) that will take all his blood out of his body, thin it down and then put it back in."

There were more words than this, but it's difficult to recall them now.

"What does this mean?" I remember thinking. The potential side effects alone were enough for us to have said no. I was scared beyond comprehension, but at this point it was all we had. We had some hope.

When terrible things happen to us, there is no right or wrong way to deal with it. At this time, you do what you feel will get you through. Being in a strange place, away from friends and family, was heart-breaking. Our other children remained at home, just for a while, with my parent, and we were alone with Oliver. We had a fight on our hands, and I had no idea at this point how big a fight it was about to be. However, our hope and optimism were short-lived, and Oliver died when he was just nine weeks old. He had been with us long enough to fill our hearts with love and joy, but also with such great sadness, more than we had ever imagined, when we had to say goodbye.

If anything positive can come from losing a child, the least you will receive is some form of peace in your life. Life will never be the same. You will be a different person and your perception of life changes. You will lose friends, and your family may avoid you – harsh but true. But that's not saying they are being mean – it may just be they don't know how to handle the situation. That isn't your problem. Time, they say, is a healer. But is it? Is it really? I think you just find a way to adapt.

I believe we are here for a short time and during this time we should try to live our lives in the best way we can – live our best lives. When we are faced with trauma or difficulties, it can be easy to fall into a trap of, "Why me? Why did this happen, or why is this happening, to me?" But the truth is that bad things happen to lots of people. In contrast, lots of amazing things happen too. My life has dealt me some blows, but I am an eternal optimist – I take any positives from these situations and turn them into lessons that I have learned, and I have grown from these experiences.

A turning point – at the age of 38, I was in a job I enjoyed. I didn't love it, but I enjoyed it. A chance conversation with a colleague about returning to education made me question whether this could be something that would be for me. I was curious. I had wanted to go to university after school, but on reflection it just wasn't the right time for me. I was in the trap of "I'm not good enough," or "I'm not the university type" – how wrong could I have been.

I researched opportunities and found an access to higher education course that would enable me to apply for university, should I pass. Again, I felt fear as I approached the local college for my entry test. I sat in a class for the first time in more than 20 years. I passed! I attended an interview and before I knew it, I was starting my academic career. I was now an achiever.

I applied for a bachelor's course at Glamorgan University to study nutrition, and I got in. Again, fear raised its ugly head. However, at this point, I faced fear with determination and a will to succeed. I worked hard and achieved a 2:1.

From my success as an undergraduate and a will to learn, I knew I had found something I was good at and something that drove me to pursue a passion for learning. I enrolled on to a further course and gained a postgraduate diploma in entrepreneurship. I met some incredible people. My confidence grew, and I realised my value – I knew that my father would have been so very proud of me. I still think of his strength and determination whenever I feel a little scared or unsure of myself.

Losing people changes us and if we can remind ourselves of the many positive experiences that we have shared with lost loved ones, I feel it gets us through even the toughest of times. I attribute my fighting spirit to growing up in a home with a father who had spina bifida and immeasurable courage. He was also an amputee. Nothing fazed him. My father fought hard when diagnosed with cancer in his later life. I was heartbroken when he lost his battle during my second year of university.

I was not a confident person when I was growing up. I was shy and lacked any form of self-confidence. My life experiences to date, good and bad, have helped me to develop into the person I am today. Gaining my postgraduate certificate in education (PGCE) helped me transform from a shy person who feared standing up and speaking in front of people, to being able to lead a class, inspire a group or just engage at networking events. I now use my knowledge, skills and experiences to inspire and teach others. I'm not finished developing myself just yet – I still have a long way to go, and every day I learn something new about myself, my abilities, my strengths and how I can make a difference in the world around me.

Sometimes we fear things out of an internal learned behaviour. But if we fear things, how can we progress? How can we achieve and gain a greater understanding of what amazing things we may miss out on? My fears and shyness had burdened me for most of my life. And if I could give my younger self a 'talking to', I would say, "Don't sweat the small stuff," and, "Please use your time wisely and pick your battles."

I have grown to understand that not every battle needs fighting. My childhood and early adult experiences have shaped who I am now, and I am forever grateful.

Being positive is not always easy. However, if I can give any advice to others it would be: yes, bad things happen and we can't always change these things. But what my own life has shown me is that good things happen too. Learn from mistakes, gain strength from adversity and don't waste a second. Believe in your abilities and remember that success is subjective.

I know for certain that if I had not had that chance conversation about education, I wouldn't have believed I could achieve a better future for myself. Education, in a strange way, saved me. It has taken me to places I never knew existed and I have been lucky to have met some incredible people. I take nothing for granted, but I have taken strength from those who believed in me and assured me I could achieve.

In the words of Jack Black in the film *School of Rock*, "I am the cat's pyjamas." And if you are reading this, remember that you are too.

Tracy Hill

Tracy is a coffee shop owner and founder of The Cats Pyjamas Kindness Project. If there were one word to describe Tracy, it would be 'resilient'. She tackles adversities, with fight and determination, and a positive attitude.

Tracy grew up in South Wales and has transformed from a shy girl, lacking in confidence, to a self-confessed self-starter. At the age of 42 she gained a BSc honours degree, followed by a postgraduate diploma in entrepreneurship from a gendered perspective. She is an advocate for supporting women. Overcoming her lack of confidence, she attained a postgraduate certificate in education (PGCE) after finding a passion for teaching.

Her children and husband remain the most important people in her life. After losing her third child, Oliver, to a rare condition, she remains pragmatic in her approach to life challenges. Her father was, and always will be her biggest inspiration.

thecatspyjamasprojectblog.wordpress.com

thecatspyjamasproject.wordpress.com

INSPIRATIONAL WOMEN OF THE WORLD

20.
A BALANCING ACT

Vix Munro

"Life can only be understood backwards;
but it must be lived forwards."

Søren Kierkegaard

Having your financial shit together is more important than ever.
It's about financial empowerment – taking control of your money,
not it controlling you. Understanding how to manage your money
is a key piece of this. But it's only part of the picture, as your
financial reality is also a reflection of your money mindset: the
core set of beliefs we subconsciously develop about money. Most
people's attitude to money is shaped by their family background
and upbringing. I believe we all have the ability to transform
our money mindset, rewrite our money story, become financially
empowered and live our best life.

A key event in my life, and which is significant to my money story,
was the sudden death of my 35-year old mother when I was
11 years old. She went into hospital for a routine operation on
a Monday and was dead by the Friday. Death wasn't new to
me, as I'd already lost two sisters, but it still left me with a huge
void, which to this day has never been filled. It was a traumatic,

life-altering experience that caused a profound disruption to my life. My day-to-day life was never the same again. And as an 11-year-old girl, I became acutely aware of my own mortality. I'd learned that life can be unexpectedly short.

I was already a bit of a spender by that age. My reaction to a very frugal upbringing was to want things, and the little money I did receive didn't last long. So, there was already a notion of money as a scarce and limited resource. That view was compounded after my mother's death. There was then also the idea that if you didn't spend money when you had it, you may die and miss out.

Fast forward to university, where I had free rein over my finances and could spend on whatever I wanted. I spent money on things I really wanted but also on things I didn't want or didn't need. I did have a fantastic time doing it. And I wasn't even living extravagantly. After university, I travelled from New Zealand to the United Kingdom and started working in the City of London. I was earning relatively good money but spending it all. London life was about having fun; there was lots of partying and travel. Sure, I could afford it, but I had nothing to show for my time earning decent money in London.

In my late 20s, I went back to university. The spending continued, but the income didn't, or at least not to the same extent. I finished my studies in debt – not a huge amount of debt, but it felt large to me. I had a student loan, a car loan and some credit card debt. Meanwhile, my sisters back in New Zealand had bought houses and I was worried that I would get left behind.

Once I was back working, I took control of my finances and got out of debt. I also bought my first flat, though I had to borrow money for the deposit. I had to severely restrict my spending to pay back that debt. It's not something I want to have to do again.

A pivotal moment for me was my 36th birthday, when I'd lived longer than my mother had. I decided to focus on my longevity and rewrote my money story to that effect. So, while life could be short, it could also be long. And whatever life handed me, I needed to enjoy it.

I've since found a balance between spending now and saving and investing for the future. And now I manage my money in a way that works for me. I'm still all for living my best life now, but not to the detriment of my future life. I don't live a frugal life – I spend money on things I really want and that bring me joy (in a Marie Kondo kind of way). I try not to spend on things I don't need or don't want. I'm aware that the future isn't guaranteed but that there's likely to be one, and that it's likely to be a long one. I believe that money is a tool that I can use to live the life I want, now and in the future. I've found the balance that works for me – my financial G-spot.

Everyone has one – that wonderful place where life feels financially good. Where you can enjoy your current lifestyle without guilt and feel confident that you can maintain it in the future. There's no reason you can't have both. Yet, most people tend to fall on one end of the spectrum, prioritising either their current life or their future life.

I understand why many people have a 'live for today' attitude. I've been there myself. We've all heard sad stories of people who worked hard, and penny pinched to save for the future, but dropped dead before they got to enjoy it. And while it's possible that you could die tomorrow, it's not probable, unless you've been diagnosed with a terminal disease with only days to live. Instead, chances are you'll live for a long time.

The reality is that people are living longer. So, not only do you have to plan for retirement, but for a potentially long one, as you don't want to limit your options. A retirement without financial security sounds miserable to me. Who wants to spend their golden years in poverty? Research shows that current retirees who are enjoying life don't attribute it to having money, yet financial stress is one of the main reasons for people not enjoying retirement.

The financial G-spot is real – it's not a myth, though it may take a bit of time and effort to find. It's a matter of giving care and attention to the present and to the future. You need to know how much to save and invest to fund your lifestyle in the future, how much you can safely spend along the way, and ensure that both allow you to create and live the life you want.

The key steps to finding your financial G-spot are:

- Know where you are now

- Know where you want to be

- Make a financial plan

- Make it happen

And then you'll have to monitor and reassess regularly. First, begin by analysing the way you live now. Are you living your best life? What things do you love to do? Do you have sufficient funds to sustain the lifestyle you want as well as saving and investing?

Second, you need a vision for your future life and what that is likely to entail. You need to assess how much it will cost to fund your future lifestyle and how many years you may need to fund this lifestyle for. Assume you're going to live a long time. You also need to calculate how much time you have to prepare for it. This will enable you to calculate how much money you need to put aside each month for the future.

Third, you need to create a financial plan and get all your ducks in a row. Once you've calculated how much money you need to save and invest for the future, you can create a budget or spending plan. It may be that you don't have enough money coming in to fund your current life and your future life. You could reassess and downgrade your desires – you can't live a champagne life on a lemonade budget. But it's better to plan to bring in more money. After all, this is your life – why compromise.

Fourth, take action and make it happen. This is by far the most important step. All the planning is meaningless without action. This is where you need to walk the walk, get out there and commit to living your best life now and in the future. The easiest way to do this is to automate your finances. Taking care of your money can be exhausting. So, setting up direct debits for all your bills, savings and investments will save you time, simplify your life and potentially save you money too.

I'm all for living life now and spending money on the things you value and that bring you joy, and also splurging on things you really, really want. But if you do this only, then you're committing to spending your golden years in poverty. Similarly, you shouldn't short-change your life today for a good life in the future. Instead, enjoy each day as if it were your last *and* save and invest as if you were going to live for a long time. It's a delicate balancing act, but it can be done. And it feels bloody good when you get there.

Vix Munro

Vix Munro is an entrepreneur, author, money enthusiast and eternal optimist. Her background is in accountancy, economics and pricing, with a career spanning over 30 years. This includes completing a master's degree in economics and running her own business for the last 12 of those years.

Vix is passionate about money, investing and the economy. Her mission is to help women step into their financial power and become money savvy in life and in business. She believes we all have the ability to transform our money mindset, rewrite our money story and become financially empowered – and that this can be liberating, life-changing and fun.

Vix was born and raised in New Zealand. She arrived in London at the age of 23 with just £30 in her pocket, and has not looked back. She doesn't like sitting still. She loves to travel and see, taste and try new things.

www.facebook.com/moneybadassary

www.instagram.com/moneybadassary

www.moneybadassary.com

Notes

Notes

Notes

Notes

Notes

Notes

Printed in Great Britain
by Amazon

50234479R00111